Team Leadership Skills for Teens

Youth Leading Youth

Brian T. Phelps

White Stag Leadership Development Program™ is a trademark of the White Stag Association and used by permission. Situational Leadership® is a registered trademark of Leadership Studies, Inc.

ISBN: 0986438308
ISBN-13: 978-0986438301

Cover image of White Stag youth staff Tamsin Kennedy and Christian Pickler courtesy of Josh Stein.

Imagine

You're 16 years old. A girl you respect has invited you to a weekend leadership workshop. Your parents agree and you eagerly accept, but you secretly hope it's not a waste of time. When you arrive, you realize you don't know anyone except the girl who invited you.

The event starts around a campfire. There are a few talks, songs, and then the girl who invited you gives out little notebooks. She tells everyone before they go to sleep to list in the notebook five traits you want to improve in yourself and one thing you must do before you die. *This is a little weird*. You're assigned to a cabin with seven other teens. You think about the list of self-improvements for a few minutes. The only thing you must do before you die is visit Tahiti.

You're dead asleep when the girl you know suddenly shakes you awake. You're panic-stricken and confused. She tells you not to talk, to get dressed, leave your flashlight, and meet outside. You don't know why and she won't explain. *Should I go?*

The trees and clouds reveal only a few faint stars. As you walk down a narrow path, the bushes brush your arms and legs. *It must be one in the morning! Where are we going?* Your breath billows in the chilly night air and you think about your warm sleeping bag. Glow sticks in perforated cans outlined with the image of a stag barely light the way. After an eternity, you descend into a narrow canyon. A creek splashes below and leaves rustle in the cold breeze. You emerge into a grove of trees lit by the glow of a fire. Your group gathers around the burning logs.

From the dark woods behind you, a booming voice tells a story about people like yourself who over many years have followed the same path to this place. Like you, they arrived filled with hesitations and reservations, personal issues, secret fears, and hidden hopes. You are dared to follow in their footsteps, to defy mediocrity, to step up and be different. *Who are these people?*

A leader steps into the firelight. He quietly tells you that many others before you have gathered around this fire and been challenged to better themselves. Many have gone on to fulfill their greatest ambition. He invites you to join this elite group—but only if you're willing to accept this invitation to improve yourself, to put aside your self-imposed limitations, to leave your comfort zone. To become the better you. *Should I do it?*

Our modern life has been largely stripped of the rites of passage that challenge youth to make a difference. As a youth leader, you're in a position to extend that invitation. Our vision is to implant in youth a desire not just to lead, but to serve—with patience, foresight, compassion, empathy, and love. *I did and so can you.*

This book provides you with the leadership skills to get started.

Contents

Growing Teens into Teams

Getting started

This book is for groups of teens 16-18 years old and their adult leaders: their coach, 4-H or FFA leader, Kiwanis advisor, recreational leader, career advisor, camp director, teacher, religious leader, and certainly their parents.

How groups work. This book is organized around the fact that every group, including teens, go through four distinct stages as they evolve from a motley group of acquaintances into a high-performing team. This process was described by Bruce Tuckman of Ohio State University. He called his model *Forming – Storming – Norming – Performing.*

Tuckman stated that these phases are a necessary and inevitable process teams go through to grow. During these phases, group members face challenges, figure out who is in charge, tackle problems, resolve interpersonal differences, identify goals, find solutions, plan work, and deliver results. But this evolution usually happens accidentally, without any guidance or purpose.

Grow your group. Groups develop unevenly. Sometimes they grow, sometimes they blow. The skills are aligned with Tuckman's stages and assist youth with gaining competence in elementary skills that prepare them to learn complex skills. When you present these eleven skills in the specific sequence given here, you're matching what you present to the needs of the evolving team. The leadership skills improve group members existing skill set and propel them forward to the next stage of group success.

Apply a proven method. Our more than 40 years of experience have proven that presenting these eleven leadership skills in a specific sequence is successful at developing high-performance teen teams. We have found that as youth learn these eleven leadership skills in this sequence, they gain self-confidence, maturity, and self-reliance. They are able to make decisions more effectively, to evaluate risk and opportunity, communicate better, share leadership, plan, act independently, and become a leader at home and in their community. After a week of leadership camp, I have over many years heard dozens of parents ask, "What did you do to my kid?"

We strongly encourage you to follow the sequence of leadership development skills shown in the illustration on page 3.

Use the small group concept. These leadership skills in this book are based on learning methods relying on the small-group methodology of 7-9 members. If you have a larger group, subdivide them into smaller clusters.

It's well established by educational researchers that small groups allow more input from members, encourage participation, and perform with greater effectiveness. In a small group, every individual's contribution matters.

Being a teenager can be challenging. Sometimes teens find friends they click with, and sometimes they fall into a clique. When you organize your small groups, separate friends. You'll avoid cliques and factions. Youth are more likely to exceed their own expectations if there aren't people around them who already know them, who expect them to behave in a certain, well-known manner. Some resist parting with their friends. When that happens, explain to the participant the philosophy of helping each person to be their best.

To encourage teen's natural competitive spirit, give each small group a unique name. Encourage a spirited attitude by asking each group to create a flag, yell, totem, song, or other tradition that differentiates them from other teams. It may seem silly, but it works.

Plan your program. This book is intended to provide you with information needed to help you present a series of leadership development experiences. You can start with a single weekend, then multiple weekends, and later try your hand at a week-long experience. Each leadership skill describes more information than can be presented in a single learning experience.

Your goal is to provide leadership learning experiences that challenge group members to move out of their comfort zone and adopt new leadership behaviors. This book lists a series of objectives for each leadership skill. Your challenge is to choose which objectives you are presenting, and then find and tailor learning activities suitable to your group's needs.

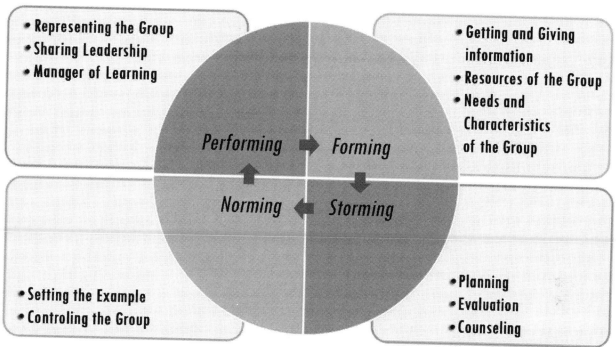

- Representing the Group
- Sharing Leadership
- Manager of Learning

Performing ➡ Forming

- Getting and Giving information
- Resources of the Group
- Needs and Characteristics of the Group

Norming ⬅ Storming

- Setting the Example
- Controling the Group

- Planning
- Evaluation
- Counseling

You can support your teen group's growth through Tuckman's stages of group growth by developing leadership skills in a specific sequence. This book describes the leadership skills; you choose the learning activities suitable to your group's needs.

Build a high performance team

Building a high performance teen team is based in part on principles allowing teens to learn on their own terms.

Encourage collaborative learning. Dozens of formal research studies have compared students taught using traditional methods to students who participate in collaborative, small groups. Youth in small groups retain information better and longer, learn more deeply, earn higher grades, are increasingly likely to graduate from high school, and improve interpersonal and communication skills.

Allow time to integrate new skills. Allow youth time to integrate what they learn and apply it in iterative steps. This may take several months.

Every teen wants to belong. Youth want to enjoy positive social relationships, learn responsibility, and earn autonomy. Youth want to be their own person. They need not only an education, but purpose and hope, skills to prosper, and the chance to take charge of their life.

Build bonds. As youth develop these leadership skills, they form strong relationships and work closely together to accomplish mutually agreed-upon tasks and goals. They evolve from a typically position-driven, hierarchal, self-centered mob of individuals to a high-performing, collaborative team who are bonded together and set and accomplish significant goals.

Have fun, make a difference. When youth make friends, they can have fun and make a difference. Use the leadership skills in this book to grow your group and everyone in it. Help them learn the skills needed to achieve their goals, today and later in life.

Use the skills in your group. Your teen group is likely engaged in other ongoing activities. Use these other pursuits to give your youth many chances to apply what they learn in their group.

Expect great things. As the leader of your leadership program, your challenge is to create conditions that over the course of your program cycle transform your group of leaderless teens into a high-performance team. You want to set high expectations for adult and youth participants alike. By expecting great things from them and helping them improve their capability as leaders, you assist a collection of individuals into becoming a high-performing team.

Stand back. Teens prosper when they are nurtured by caring adults. Not bossed. If you're an adult leader of youth, one of your biggest challenges is create conditions for learning, and then get out of the way and allow them to fail. You must abandon your protective parenting habits and learn to stand back. Your job is to be a coach, an advisor, a mentor. Not a leader. The only time you ought to directly interfere is if a teen's behavior exceeds your organization's health and safety boundaries.

Create a leaderless experience

One of the best ways to motivate your group to learn about leadership is to put them into a "leaderless experience." Soon after you've formed each small group, before they know what's going on, give each a challenging task that requires the group to communicate, collaborate, and problem solve. Then step back and watch.

Notice who takes charge, if any, and how it happens. Observe who hangs back. Study the group dynamics. Allow the group to plow forward and depending on how well they perform, interrupt their process after about 20 minutes. Debrief them on their experience. Use this opportunity to talk about leadership, why leaders exist, how leaders are chosen, and the basic skills of a leader. Ask questions to help them understand the need for leadership skills. And when they're ready, announce your leadership development plan.

Choose relevant objectives

As the Manager of Learning, whether you're a youth or an adult, choose specific objectives that meet the needs of your group during a given leadership development experience. Depending on your goals, your audience's needs and characteristics, and their maturity, adapt these skills to your youth and your organization.

Assess your participants' needs and characteristics, abilities, maturity, interest level, and readiness. Then decrease or increase the number of objectives and amount of content to meet their needs.

Consider your goals. Before you begin leadership development, establish your goals for building your team over the entire development cycle. Based on these goals, plan an appropriate amount of time to develop and provide learning experiences. The more ambitious your goals, the more time you'll need to work with participants.

Choose objectives. We've listed possible learning objectives for each of the leadership skills. Sometimes an objective includes a number as a criteria. There may be more responses that are considered valid. Increase or decrease the criteria number depending on your goals.

Choose content. A few of the eleven leadership skills are more complex than others. All of the leadership skills contain more information than a learner can absorb during a single learning activity.

Consider the individuals. The amount of information you want to include in a learning experience depends on the maturity of participants, their needs and characteristics, and your goals. Part of the content is too complex for young teens and may be more or less relevant to their needs. Break your learning sessions into segments of about an hour. Remember the mind can only absorb what the seat can endure.

Select appropriate learning activities

Select learning activities with a purpose. Use these eleven leadership skills as a framework to develop hands-on youth leadership development activities and experiences. These include games, competitions, projects, experiments, role-plays, discussions, case-studies, simulations, or whatever meets your needs. Your goal is to help individuals develop a clear understanding of how they communicate, make decisions, work together, and can improve themselves.

Keep it simple. Select learning activities that motivate your youth to learn leadership. Learning activities can be extremely simple. To encourage the need to learn Giving and Getting Information, play The Telephone Game (look it up). To motivate interest in Resources of the

Group, give them their food for the weekend and watch what happens. To boost awareness for learning Counseling, have someone pretend to be heart-broken about the end of a relationship.

Keep hands and minds busy. Abundant research shows that youth learn through multiple senses. When you offer activities that require movement, talking, and listening, you engage multiple areas of the brain. When youth actually practice a skill, they retain information better and longer.

Do your research. There are thousands of online resources, magazine articles, and books that contain activities you can adapt for your youth. Find or create the experiences that fit your group.

By using the small-group method and hands-on learning, you cover less information, but youth learn more.

Consider your group. Before preparing a learning session, assess your group's needs and characteristics along with your goals. Consider what you want to cover in the time available. If you're overly ambitious and cram too much into a learning experience, you'll overwhelm them. On the other hand, your assessment of what they already know may be wrong. They might be ready for more information. It's always a good idea to prepare to deliver extra information.

Design your learning program

Select your learning objectives. The number and complexity of the objectives you choose determine how much time you need for your development program. Select objectives from among those listed in each leadership skill. If you need to add your own, make sure your objectives are specific, measurable, achievable, realistic, and time-bound ("SMART").

Select conference dates. The learners in your program have probably already been selected as leaders or have shown an interest in learning about leadership. When you're organized and prepared, start developing their leadership skills over a series of one- or two-day development conferences. Once you've proven to yourself these work, you may choose to plan a week-long learning conference.

Prepare each learning session. The American Society for Training and Development reports that professional trainers need about 40 hours of preparation for each hour of traditional classroom training. This number emphasizes that preparing learning experiences requires significant thought and preparation.

Fortunately, this book contains your learning objectives. If you're already familiar with planning and preparing a workshop, working with youth, and participatory learning methods, you are well positioned to get started. So depending on how ambitious your goals are, allow a minimum of five to ten hours to prepare learning sessions for each hour of actual team development.

Become familiar with the leadership skills, prepare an outline of what you'll cover, identify and gather the resources needed, and plan the learning session. Develop learning sessions that include an organized description of the key learning points, activities, resources, and time you'll use to guide your group toward specific learning objectives.

Plan your leadership workshops. It takes planning and preparation to deliver a series of leadership development experiences. To develop your group's leadership skills and build an effective team, plan on at least 125 to 150 workshop hours, or from 6-10 weekends over as many months.

If you are able to meet more often, consider condensing the schedule to two workshops a month, but this is usually a challenge for active, busy, youth leaders. There is also sizable benefit to allowing participants time between meetings to absorb and practice what they learned during the prior workshop. They also need time to complete assignments you give them.

You also need to manage logistics like feeding people, finding workshop locations, medical screenings, adult background checks, parental permission forms, transportation, sleeping accommodations, and so forth.

If you are an adult advisor or leader of youth, the good news is you don't have to do this yourself. Use these necessities as learning experiences and give these challenges to the teens.

Examples:

- Individual's dietary needs figure into the leadership skill Needs and Characteristics of the group.

- Finding someone who is an able cook is part of the leadership skill Resources of the Group.

- Getting all the food bought and brought to the learning event—and then cooking it!—is a requirement for the leadership skill planning.

Develop a budget. Depending on your organization and the resources they offer, program expenses vary. Your costs include supplies like flip charts and markers, site costs, snacks and meals, and membership fees. You may receive income from participant fees, donations, scholarships, and grants.

Plan your time. Everyone's time is precious and it's challenging to get people together at the same time. The time you have to conduct learning activities is precious. To make effective use of their time, use a learning method that maximizes the development process.

Be a Manager of Learning. Use the Manager of Learning methodology to build highly effective teams and to structure your learning experiences. The Manager of Learning methodology is a system for iterative learning and a process for involving youth in building effective teams. It's a design for producing in-depth learning.

Focus on learning. Manager of Learning is both one of the competencies taught in the program and a system for leadership development. It is a participatory, experiential approach you use throughout your entire program to design and implement leadership development.

The Manager of Learning leadership competency is a complex subject. The ability to help others develop this skill requires repeated exposure and practice.

There are six steps to the Manager of Learning methodology.

Guided discovery. Present the learners with a pre-designed, hands-on activity that requires them to demonstrate their skill in the topic of the learning session. This helps them recognize what they know—and what they don't know. It reveals exactly what topics to include in—and remove from—the Teach / Learn step of the Manager of Learning cycle.

State your objectives. Tell your learners what you want them to learn. Based on what you glean during the guided discovery, add or subtract specific objectives and content from your learning plan.

Teach / Learn. Here's where you fill the gaps between what they already know and what you want them to know when you finish. This is based on your goals and objectives. Your goal is to facilitate a fun, hands-on learning experience.

Application. Create a situation that requires the learners to apply what they learned. If appropriate, you may choose to repeat the guided discovery as the application.

Evaluation. Ask the learners to assess whether or not they completed the objectives you gave at the beginning of the learning activity.

Perform. Help participants put what they've learned to work in the group and in real life. Give them time to write down plans to apply the leadership skills. Have them write down specific criteria they can use to measure progress.

Manager of Learning is a simple, iterative, cyclical system method you use to expose learners to the need to know and involve them in their own learning. Repeat a learning experience more than once, and with each repetition, alter and enhance the information to meet the learners' needs.

For details, see Manager of Learning on page 195.

Select a service project

As you present these leadership skills over a period of several months, your group matures and begins to perform at a high level. Now they need a challenging experience that allows them to put their skills to work. They are ready to perform.

Find an audacious service project. Now the team (no longer merely a group) is ready for an opportunity to make a difference: challenge them to complete a hairy, audacious service project. The project needs to be complex, require several weeks of preparation and planning, and involve other members of the community.

Service learning gives you a chance to work on real-world problems. You set goals, apply critical thinking, problem-solve, make decisions, and communicate. Taking part in an extended service project allows you to use your leadership skills to find real solutions to actual problems. By working with community members and leaders, you gain self-sufficiency, interpersonal and social skills, and self-esteem.

Examples. In Syracuse, New York, youth from the Beard Alternative School built and maintained a flower and vegetable garden on the city's southwest side. At Britton's Neck High School in Gresham, South Carolina, youth obtained property from a community member and built a fire station. Youth at the White River High School in Buckley, Washington developed a stream-monitoring program to improve the habitat for the endangered Chinook King Salmon.

Other examples include rehabilitating a run-down park, hosting a Special Olympics, building bat houses, providing social activities for senior citizens, developing an oral history project, and developing and presenting leadership development programs for other youth.

To learn more, see *Perform* on page 228.

Evaluate and iterate. At the project's conclusion, assist the youth with an evaluation of what they learned and gained from their efforts. If possible, persuade community leaders to recognize the youth and their success. After celebrating their achievements, challenge them to find areas for improvement, gaps in their knowledge, skills, and attitude. Now take another look at the leadership skill objectives and plan a new series of learning activities that raise the bar for your team members.

For more information about choosing learning activities, see *Manage the learning experience* on page 213.

About these leadership skills

These eleven leadership skills describe a specific set of knowledge, skills, and attitudes that comprise an integrated framework for acquiring leadership ability. These skills condense the essential elements of leading into language and ideas that are useful to and understandable by youth.

Conceived by Dr. Béla Bánáthy. The skills described in this book are based on the original work of systems scientist and educator Dr. Béla Bánáthy. After the end of World War II, and after spending six years in a displaced persons camp, Bánáthy was hired in 1958 as a Hungarian language instructor at the Army Language School in Monterey, California. There he renewed his interest in Scouting and leadership development.

Origins in White Stag program. With the support of the Monterey Bay Area Council of the Boy Scouts of America, Bánáthy founded a youth leadership development program that he named "White Stag," after the mythical emblem of the Hungarian people. This same emblem was the symbol of the 4th World Jamboree held in Hungary in 1933, which Bánáthy attended as a 14 year old youth.

Designed for youth. Bánáthy designed his program to meet the needs of youth from 11 to 17 years of age. He did this when leadership theory was still in its infancy and before researchers had clearly identified the specific needs of youth for leadership education.

The leadership curriculum of the White Stag program was later adapted by the National Council of the Boy Scouts of America for both its adult Wood Badge and junior leader development programs.

Bánáthy sowed the seeds of leadership development, and thousands have reaped the benefits of his work. Many of these individuals have contributed directly and indirectly to sustaining and growing the White Stag program, and all are contributors to refining our understanding of the competencies of leadership.

Current uses. The White Stag Leadership Development program is currently comprised of two volunteer-led, non-profit charitable organizations in California. The adult leaders are interested parents and community members. They come from a variety of backgrounds including business owners, machinists, real estate agents, computer scientists, educators, lawyers, physicians, day care workers, and more.

These two programs have sustained and nurtured the idea of youth leadership development since 1958. The two programs do not have executive staff nor the time or funds necessary to join larger organizations, publish papers, or attend conferences. White Stag has largely remained out of the limelight of academic and professional youth leadership development organizations in the United States.

The White Stag program is unique among youth leadership programs. Attendees come from all over the western United States, Mexico, China, and Taiwan. The week-long summer camp experience is planned and conducted entirely by youth with minimal adult oversight. Many youth staff devote 10 full weekends a year to staff development activities. White Stag is a three-phase, nine-level program. This structure allows youth to return as they mature and learn more each year. White Stag is fun with a purpose, packed with activities, games, and challenging activities including hiking and camping in the backcountry. It is full of spirit and tradition in the form of symbolism, stories, patches, campfires, yells, songs, personal reflection, and ceremonies.

The two groups have since the program's founding trained more than 25,000 youth in the eleven competencies of leadership. Their grass-roots effort is a model worth emulation.

To learn to lead, youth need to practice. Use the skills in this book as the basis for choosing learning activities. These include panel discussions, quizzes, buzz groups, projects, experiments, role-plays, discussions, case-studies, simulations, or whatever works for you.

The events should be a challenging experience for your youth. Start small, evaluate, and continuously improve. Add bigger challenges and expand your horizons.

Focus on learning, not teaching

The most important element of this approach to teen leadership development is the focus on learning, not teaching. As adults who work with youth, we need to shift our attention from what we're teaching to what the youth are learning. It's a subtle but important distinction.

Unlike school. In typically rigid, linear teaching situations (like school!), the learner reacts to the teacher's active role. The teacher selects the content and experience; the learner reacts to them. The teacher organizes information for the learner, who passively consumes it. The teacher is not encouraged to consider the learner's unique motives or needs.

Focus on the learner. In an open system, the learning presenter must be adaptable, flexible, and responsive to the learner's needs. When learning is the true focus, rigid scheduling and time tables are eliminated. The focus is no longer on checking off a list of learning activities, but on what the learners gain. The focus isn't on your satisfaction as an instructor in completing a lesson, but on what the learner gains from the experience.

The learner chooses what they learn. The learner plays an active role in selecting the content that is presented. This is done by engaging them in a discovery process that allows both them and you to find out what they already know.

Example: You may find out during a learning experience that participants already know a portion of what you intend to cover. Modify your objectives and planned activities immediately, during the learning experience. Don't wait until next time!

A simple model

Many knowledgeable, respected authors have written volumes striving to capture and define leadership.

Room for growth. This book isn't a final answer. The essential skills of teen leadership continue to evolve. We're responsive to change in the needs of our communities. Our understanding of leadership grows as research and practice alters our concept of the function of the leader and of leadership. Add to and update this body of knowledge as needed, as we have yet to find a leadership behavior that doesn't fit within this eleven competency model.

We hope youth use these competencies to become better leaders. These core leadership skills represent our best thinking at this time, but they are not by any means complete. Those of us who have inherited Bánáthy's approach to learning remain open to new ideas that complement our understanding of leadership.

Change is expected. The ongoing march of change doesn't remove the need for a clear statement of what youth leadership is. Our goal is to describe leadership skills in simple terms that youth understand. They must be able to practice and apply the behaviors that qualify as leadership. These skills are a foundation for youth to learn leadership attitudes, skills, and knowledge for their entire life.

A systems approach. These skills are a systems approach to learning leadership. Bánáthy designed this approach to be multi-directional. This means the model not only allows feedback, but it also has feed-ahead or feed-forward strategies for improving learning experiences. This allows you, for example, to apply learning from an earlier step in the learning experience to a later step.

Enhance people's potential. Bánáthy encouraged individuals in the White Stag program to think for themselves, to apply their learning wherever it's applicable—not only in the White Stag program he founded. He wanted participants to learn to live together in harmony and to be able to pool their learning, when necessary, to perform as team members and accomplish tasks they can't do by themselves. We encourage learners to strive to reach their greatest potential as people.

Born leaders are a myth

In the early industrial age, society assumed leadership was a trait you were born with. As sociologists and scientists studied employees, managers, and the companies they worked for, they learned more about human interaction. Society gradually began to understand that leadership is a product of the situation and the people involved.

Leadership is shared. Most people think that one person in a group is the leader. While there is usually a designated leader—someone appointed or elected to the role—leadership responsibility may shift as needed from one member to another. Any member of a group may possess the knowledge, skill, or ability needed by the team to achieve its goals at a particular point in time.

Whatever your age, you are a leader. A 12 year old may want to play a different game, a 24 year old may want a better job, and a 64 year old may want a better retirement. Before the Industrial Revolution, a single person could build a boat or a house. Today, everyone has to interact with others to succeed. Whatever your age, you have opportunities to lead.

Leadership is situational. Depending on the group, someone is likely exerting more influence than anyone else at any given moment. In school, at home, in clubs, organizations, and government—in all personal and business contexts—leadership is influenced by the needs of the job and the group.

Become a multi-disciplinary leader. A few individuals excel in a selected leadership roles but neglect others. Women and men who are recognized and acclaimed as outstanding leaders have cultivated excellent skills in many areas. These multi-disciplinary leaders adapt their leadership style to the maturity of the group, to match individual needs, and to the situation.

Let's uncomplicate leadership

There are dozens of organizations across the United States and in other countries that claim to train youth in something they call leadership. The overly-sophisticated theories and ideas applied to developing youth leadership is dumbfounding.

Academics. College professors and graduate students grind out academic papers an average youth and even adult leaders have a hard time understanding. Unfortunately, the educator's good intentions too often only confuse those they intend to reach.

Professional organizations. A few companies charge thousands of dollars to allow youth to live in a college dorm, visit historical sites, role-play historical figures, and learn about government. Others put a proprietary stamp on their concept of leadership development, unnecessarily complicating it, but allowing them to charge premium prices.

Proprietary programs. In an effort to brand and differentiate themselves, consultants, agencies, and organizations routinely create new programs, invent new ideas, coin new acronyms, and host new seminars. Everyone wants a piece of the funding pie. Despite these challenges, these programs gain traction, but they tend to remain regionalized and marginalized.

A simple definition. Leadership is easy to define.

Leadership is the ability to keep the group together and get the job done.

This is our simple goal.

Leadership builds the person

This book helps you learn to influence and contribute to individual and team success. As you develop as an individual, the entire team benefits. As the team grows, its members gain new abilities.

Learning leadership is a life-long process. When you learn leadership skills, you improve your interpersonal skills, self-esteem, confidence, and social skills. By beginning leadership development early in life, you learn that personal growth is life-long.

All of the top achievers I know are life-long learners... Looking for new skills, insights, and ideas. If they're not learning, they're not growing... not moving toward excellence. –Denis Waitley

Learning leadership skills like planning before you complete high school gives you tremendous advantages over many of your peers. When you are aware of the need to understand the needs and characteristics of the group, or how to share leadership, or plan a project, you are in a unique positon to grow your organization.

Practice, fail, and correct. By taking part in realistic, hands-on learning activities, you get to practice leadership. You learn that failure and mistakes is a necessary hiccup on the path to success, and not an error to be avoided at all costs. You get to attempt new ways of leading in a safe environment where mistakes are rewarded with evaluation, the opportunity to correct and improve, and growth.

Adult mentorship. Ideally, you are supported by adults who mentor the youth, quickly spot problems, give feedback, correct, and manage continued improvement. Adult mentorship and coaching is critical to helping you gain increased confidence before experiencing the challenge of a real situation.

It's what you learn after you know it all that counts. —John Wooden

Why leadership for youth

As youth demonstrate maturity and readiness, society needs to empower them to assume additional responsibility, accountability, and authority. To make this possible, society must make the vocabulary and skills of leadership accessible and widely available to youth.

As you invest in youth and enable them to lead, you build self-esteem, self-confidence, and individual capabilities that last a lifetime. You're helping individuals become better parents, business owners, community members, and effective citizen leaders.

Adulthood is too late

Adults can choose today from hundreds of different programs, seminars, and courses that claim to teach leadership primarily to adults.

Leadership courses are expensive. Many companies offer employees formal training to develop their management skills. In the United States during 2012, tens of thousands of companies paid over $162.4 billion to send thousands of employees to training. During 2013, the cost of training averaged $1,208 per employee.

If you're fortunate enough as an adult to attend a management development course, you're still facing a significant hurdle: your co-workers and managers likely aren't there.

If you're an adult, maybe your company is one of the few that offers a tuition reimbursement program. That allows you, on your own time, to find classes and get reimbursed, but usually only if the class is related to what you do on the job. Forget about personal development courses.

Adult training is isolated. There are thousands of consultants and advisors who make tens of thousands and even millions of dollars annually selling organizational development services to companies. These organizational development workshops are typically focused on structuring work and helping individuals to contribute to their company's success. If you get something out of the experience that applies to your personal life, that's great, but the employer isn't usually too concerned about that.

Personal growth is expensive. Individuals spend millions of dollars each year pursuing personal growth. Self-improvement is a $10 billion a year industry in the United States. In self-help seminars that fill hotel ball rooms and convention centers across the nation, tens of thousands of adults fork over millions of dollars yearly to feel effective and empowered.

Attendees get pumped full of desire, injected with a positive mental attitude, and strive to live life more creatively, act enthusiastically, feel successful, and create added happiness and wealth. No matter that most of the self-help gurus can't provide any solid evidence that their programs actually do any good.

But both the company-sponsored programs and the individual seminars leave you with the same problem: you're usually on your own. When you get back to work, or return home, your co-workers, your managers, and your family and friends are unlikely to understand and support the new ideas—the new you—that you bring back.

Adult leadership development is late. Lastly, leadership development efforts for adults are often belated. If an adult is lucky enough to attend a leadership training course, they still have one huge strike against them: they have a lot to unlearn. Their thinking, expectations, and habits are unfortunately usually well set and conditioned.

Communities in need

Our communities and nations are hurting for effective leaders. Today's youth are tomorrow's leaders.

Youth learn and adapt. It's well established that youth learn more quickly than adults. Leadership development must start during the formative years of youth, when they're ready and eager to learn. Youth need to be better prepared to meet the many present and emerging challenges in our communities and countries.

Youth are impatient. Teens are often impatient with the slow, linear pace of traditional pedagogy found in schools. They dislike sitting still. They want to be involved in meaningful, participative activities. They want to leadership skills they can use today and tomorrow.

Youth want respect. They want to be treated with respect, not human test tubes to be stuffed with information. They don't need to be programmed to become employees, but encouraged to prosper. They don't want to be prevented from going bad, they want to be challenged to get ahead. They don't want to be patronized, or talked down to, but lifted up.

Youth want to be engaged. Youth yearn to learn in ways that engage their mind, bodies, and hearts. They don't want to study abstract concepts, they need practical solutions.

Leadership is the capacity to translate vision into reality. —Warren G. Bennis

School isn't the answer

Traditional schools are usually well-equipped to teach children the basics of academic success. But they are woefully unprepared and are fundamentally unable to develop leadership except in the most rudimentary fashion.

Leadership class isn't. Many high schools have "leadership classes," but these are only available to the few students who are elected to the student council. These students are typically already leaders among their peers.

Schools often state that the intent is for student participants to learn about democracy and leadership. But many so-called leadership classes are merely bureaucratic extensions of the school administration and teach students how to organize events like Homecoming and sell tickets.

Faculty advisors and coaches. Youth who participate in school clubs or sports may be fortunate to be taught by a talented advisor or coach. The adult helps the youth gain leadership experience as a member or leader of a team.

Unfortunately, the faculty advisor who volunteers—or is assigned —as the advisor typically has little experience as a leader and no background in leadership education.

So the leadership education a student receives in school is largely happenstance and entirely dependent on the quality of the available faculty.

What youth need now

Many experts have tried to figure out what youth need to become effective adults. Donna Lopiano, the former Executive Director of the Women's Sports Foundation, wrote that society needs to give youth "training and instruction so that they can improve their basic people skills, organizational skills, and communication skills."

Good habits formed at youth make all the difference. —Aristotle

National youth experts on leadership. At a meeting of youth advocates from across the United States in 2007, Hare and Richards (*Blazing the Trail: A New Direction in Youth Development & Leadership* - 2007) described how participants decided to differentiate between youth development and youth leadership.

They found that:

Youth Development *is a process which prepares young people to meet the challenges of adolescence and adulthood through a coordinated, progressive series of activities and experiences which help them to become socially, morally, emotionally, physically, and cognitively competent. Positive youth development addresses the broader developmental needs of youth, in contrast to deficit-based models that focus solely on youth problems.*

Youth Leadership, they agreed, has two primary characteristics:

The ability to guide or direct others on a course of action, influence the opinion and behavior of other people, and show the way by going in advance. (Teaching Self-Determination to Students with Disabilities: Basic Skills for Successful Transition - 1998)

The ability to analyze one's own strengths and weaknesses, set personal and vocational goals, and have the self-esteem to carry them out. It includes the ability to identify community resources and use them, not only to live independently, but also to establish support networks to participate in community life and to affect positive social change. (Adolescent Employment Readiness Center, Children's Hospital, n.d.)

Formative experiences. In addition to striving to agree on what it means to help youth develop and become leaders, a number of researchers have identified needs of youth for specific types of formative experiences. In a well-regarded study, Ferber, Pittman, and Marshall (*State Youth Policy: Helping all Youth to Grow up Fully Prepared and Fully Engaged* - 2002) described five developmental priorities for youth:

Learning: developing positive basic and applied academic attitudes, skills, and behaviors.

Thriving: developing physically healthy attitudes, skills, and behaviors.

Connecting: developing positive social attitudes, skills, and behaviors.

Working: developing positive vocational attitudes, skills, and behaviors.

Leading: developing positive civic attitudes, skills, and behaviors.

Successful program characteristics. Another study identified characteristics of programs that help youth acquire the attitudes, skills, and knowledge required to be effective in society (*Youth Development & Youth Leadership. A Background Paper* - 2004). These include:

- Strong relationships with adults

- Develop skills in mediation, conflict resolution, team dynamics, and project management

- New roles and responsibilities based on experiences and resources that provide opportunity for growth

- Teamwork and peer networking

- Opportunities to practice communication, negotiation, and refusal skills

We encourage you to reflect on what these professional educators have found. Our experience has shown that their conclusions have merit. Your goal is to create a program that addresses these needs. It's not easy, but it's extraordinarily rewarding!

Help your community

The real measure of leadership excellence is evident when you act based on what's best for your team. As you mature, you recognize that the community around you is part of your team, and you have a role as a responsible member of that community.

Leaders of highly effective teams put the community's goals ahead of personal needs and recognition. As a leader, you know that supporting the community is a priority and encourage your team to work together for the common good. You don't have to love each member of your team or your community, but the team is more important than any individual or differences between them.

This book is a start. Combine your group's current program and interests with the leadership skills found here. Add learning activities that match the needs and characteristics of your group. Apply what you learn about leadership at home, in school, and in your community. Now, you're ready to start making a difference.

Forming the Group

When a group initially gathers, members are usually meeting each other for the first time.

Form relationships. Everyone has questions and expectations. The group members learn who is in the group, individual and group needs, what they have in common, and their differences. They clarify expectations and responsibilities.

They socialize to learn about each other. They look for clues about each other's identities. They gather first impressions based on dress, language, and attitude. They learn about schools attended, where group members live, friends in common, and hobbies.

This doesn't mean that every member of the group suddenly feels buddy-buddy with everyone, but you've started the process.

Identify group goals. Using learning activities that support the group's goals. Start by defining short-term objectives and activities that focus on the group's purpose.

Depending on the nature of the group, there's group house-keeping, like meals, planning the next meeting, deciding where to meet, carpools, and so forth. You may need to alert members to specific standards inherent in the parent organization, like a buddy system, dress or language standards, or sleeping arrangements if you're staying overnight.

Identify the leader. Most importantly, group members figure out how they are led. A few people may quickly attempt to dominate the group. Everyone looks at each other through a web of personal filters, figuring out their place in the group and how they can accomplish their goals.

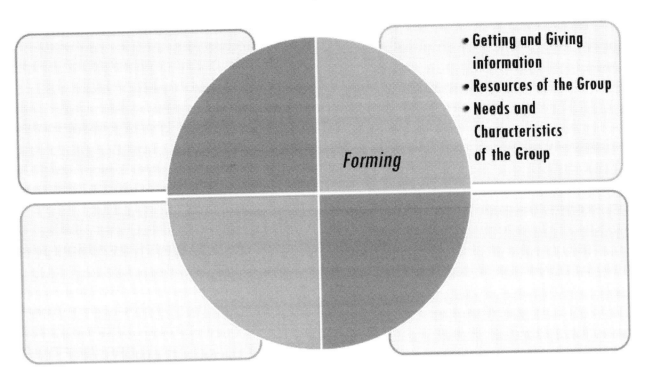

Forming

- **Getting and Giving information**
- **Resources of the Group**
- **Needs and Characteristics of the Group**

As the group forms, they figure out how to communicate and who they are. You want to help them evolve from a collection of unrelated individuals striving to figure out what they're doing into a team who are banded together for a purpose.

This "getting started" process must be at least partially repeated if new members join the group at any time, because new members alter interpersonal dynamics and relationships. These new members are also unfamiliar with the group's goals and purpose.

The task. They learn about what brought them together, their purpose, communication channels. They ask questions about the task.

They find out about the scope of the task, its place within the larger frame of work, the resources available to accomplish it, and the time given.

Form the group. To support forming the group, create learning experiences that develop group member's knowledge of the first three competencies:

- **Giving and Getting Information**. The essential skill necessary to be an effective leader is to give and receive information accurately.

- **Resources of the Group**. Know and capitalize on group members' attitude, skills, and knowledge.

- **Needs and Characteristics of the Group**. Understand what makes your team members tick: what motivates them, how to meet their needs, how to support their growth.

Giving and Getting Information

About Giving and Getting Information

When people first join a group, they need to learn about the nature of the group and the task. Nothing happens until they figure out how they're going to communicate, what they need to communicate about, and their resources, purpose, goals, and direction.

Each member makes a series of decisions, consciously and unconsciously, about their role in the group. You need to guide the group through this process. He wants to inspire, inform, persuade, unite, motivate, and direct the group. Communicate within the group to build a team, and outside the group, to gain additional resources and to seek cooperation from other groups.

Communication is a two-way street. While you think you know what you said, others may have received it quite differently.

I know what I have given you. I do not know what you received. —Antonio Porchia

The ability to communicate effectively is one of the most important skills of leadership—not only what you communicate, but how. The success or failure of your group rises or falls on Giving and Getting Information. You are constantly on call to get and give information. Your ability to communicate makes or breaks your group's success.

Giving and Getting Information is essential to group success. Nothing happens until the group has established effective communication on multiple levels. As a leader, begin developing the group's skills in communication as a way to get the group going. Choose activities that require the group to communicate in ways that stretch their skills and abilities.

For example, right after the group has initially gathered, ask for a "representative of the group" to step aside with you. Then orally give that person a meaningful, complex task for the group to perform. Evaluate the group's performance with them afterward—especially their communication skills—and help them develop and improve. Now you're on your way to building a team.

As individuals grow to understand what the group and its members is about, they identify the group norms and group goals. They make an informed decision about whether to join the group. This helps maintain group membership. Individuals are able to call on other members' knowledge, skills and abilities, increasing the likelihood that the task at hand is completed.

All of this happens through communication in one form or another.

Objectives

When you complete presenting the content in this chapter, learners are able to:

- List two ways to encourage open communication.
- Name three types of interpersonal communication methods.
- List three ways to speak assertively and make sure others understand your concerns.
- List two ways to resolve differences when someone refuses to agree to a decision.
- List two ways to use body language to improve communication when presenting information.
- List three ways you to project your ideas to improve communication.
- List four ways to use your voice effectively when communicating.
- List three disadvantages of using acronyms.
- List one advantage of using acronyms.
- List three characteristics of effective corrective feedback.
- Name the five senses and demonstrate how to use at least three of the five senses to transmit information.
- List four techniques for giving information clearly.
- Define two steps of reflective listening.

- List three characteristics of reflective listening.
- List four behaviors that let people know that you're listening.
- List five behaviors that block effective communication.
- List the two senses used most often to receive information.
- List two factors you control when giving information.
- List two ways a recipient controls the information they're receiving.
- List five ways to remember and retrieve information so that it isn't forgotten or distorted.
- List three techniques for taking notes.
- List three ways a leader helps the group succeed during meetings.
- List three reasons to prepare flip charts in advance.
- List two advantages of using flip charts during a meeting or discussion.

Imagine

You and a few friends from school all like camping and hiking. At the beginning of the school year, you decide to form a hiking club so you can invite more people to join. One of your members knows a teacher who likes to hike and he volunteers to be your advisor.

At your first meeting after school, the teacher had a last-minute problem and can't attend. Your friends show up and so does a dozen other people you don't know. Everyone messes around. It's hard to get anything done. No one is in charge. One person you know from Algebra class leaves. Two guys who are on the football team start bragging about a hard hike they did together last year. They practically take over the meeting as they talk about the hike.

One of your friends, a girl who is the volleyball team captain, finally gets everyone's attention. She asks everyone to introduce themselves and tell how much experience they have camping and backpacking. The two football players get a little miffed that no one wants to listen to them anymore and make a noisy exit. You wonder if this club idea was such a good idea after all.

The volleyball team captain gets everyone to sign a list with their contact information. She asks everyone to pitch in ideas about where they would like to on a first hike. One member of the group is certified as a rock climber. He knows about a camping spot with nearby rock-climbing spots. Everyone likes his idea. The group picks a date for next month.

During the campout, the certified rock climber says his little brother has friends who haven't been camping. He says he wants to take them on a camp out. He knows the owner of the local camping supply store and is sure he'll donate used camping gear. Several of your friends like this idea. They agree to get together and to organize a campout for the kids.

Your hiking club just grew into something bigger. Is it okay that the volleyball team captain took over like she did? Now make a few decisions. You nickname your idea "Kamping for Kids." But a campout for kids who don't have any experience is complicated. You have to coordinate transportation, food, and equipment. Who's going to do that? Who's going to invite the kids? Who do you need to get permission from to do this event? Who's going to keep track of everything that's going on? How are you going to communicate with everyone?

Two-way communication

This leadership skill is called *Giving and Getting Information* and not *Communication*. Sometimes people want to call it "Communication," but there are reasons to use the specific name.

Communication. "Communication" describes all types of kinds of ways to exchange information. This includes talking, but texting, television, telephone, letters, Instagram, and even Snapchat.

Giving and Getting Information. This leadership skills describes specific interactive, two-way, interpersonal methods for individuals to exchange information. This interpersonal process includes:

- What the sender intended to communicate and how they communicated it.

- What was understood by the recipient and how it was received.

Both the sender and the recipient consciously and unconsciously influence communication.

Sender's impact on communication. The sender's loudness, attitude, body language, tone, and even cultural bias affect the content of their communication.

Recipient's impact on communication. The recipient responds to the sender's conscious and unconscious content. The recipient hears words, but they also observe body language, tone of voice, and other behaviors. The recipient isn't a blank slate. He may be tired, bored, and even biased. These influence what the recipient hears and how he interprets what he hears and understands.

To verify that information was communicated accurately, both the sender and recipient need to clarify and verify.

Create a positive atmosphere

You want to encourage open communication and minimize the chances that listeners misunderstand your message.

List two ways to encourage open communication.

You facilitate communication happen by following a few simple ground rules.

Use their name. People love to hear their name. Verify that the learner is paying attention and call them by name. If you're presenting information to people you don't know well, use a cheat sheet: write their names down on a seating chart where you can refer to it during your learning session.

Discourage cross-talk. Show respect for everyone's ideas. Don't allow comments that put down someone else's ideas.

Record ideas in front of the team. Write contributions down on a flip chart or whiteboard where everyone sees them. Have someone convert what is recorded to notes to make sure nothing is lost.

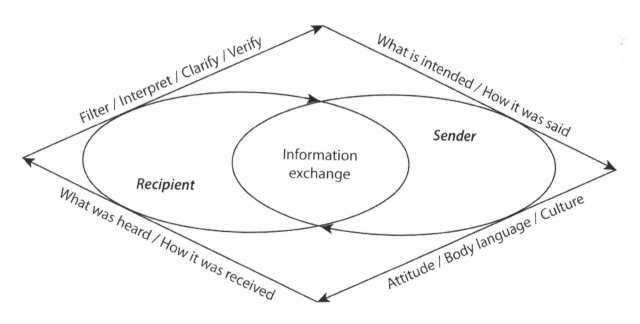

The cycle of Giving and Getting Information

Show appreciation for contributions. Let everyone know that you appreciate their ideas with statements like, "That's great!"

Use your communication channels

Name three types of interpersonal communication methods.

To improve communication, use a variety of communication channels. People primarily exchange information using three types of communication.

Verbal. Oral communication is real-time, person-to-person or voice-to-voice conversations that allow immediate feedback and interchange.

Written. Written communication is exchanging information in various written forms, including notes, charts, illustrations, maps and more.

Non-verbal. Non-verbal communication is influenced by proximity to the listener. It includes hand gestures, facial expressions, inflection, pitch, tone, eye contact, and even touch.

When you interact with others, you gain information both passively, by observing without asking questions, and actively, by directly engaging others. You're attempting to gain information that allows you to interact more effectively. If you understand people's needs and characteristics, you're better able to predict how they think, feel, and act, and to lead them.

Be heard

While verbal communication appears to be straightforward, it's not. You may be having a hard time saying what you think or feel. Sometimes you feel like people aren't listening to you. This leads to serious misunderstandings, resentment, hurt feelings, and blocks a group's progress. And because what you say isn't always what the recipient hears.

List three ways to speak assertively and make sure others understand your concerns.

Sometimes it's necessary to use an assertive tone and manner to persuade people to pay attention. Speaking assertively means to speak forcefully in neither a submissive nor aggressive manner so people understand your meaning.

There are several ways to encourage others to listen to your concerns.

Speak for yourself. To avoid putting others on the defense, use the word "I". This also indicates that you own your feelings and aren't blaming them on someone else.

Maintain eye contact. Looking someone in the eye shows that you are sincere. Allow natural breaks in eye contact during unimportant parts of the conversation. Don't start a staring contest because this creates hostility and tension.

Use body language. Sit upright and push your shoulders back. This reinforces the impression that you're sincere. Use gestures that invite people to collaborate, like an open palm, smiles, and circular arm movements.

Speak plainly. Say what you mean as simply and clearly as possible. Describe the facts as accurately as possible. This isn't the time to avoid dealing with a problem. Use an even and moderate tone of voice. Don't use foul language.

Speak up but don't yell. If you speak too quietly, people may not take you seriously. If you yell, you risk increasing tension, and people respond to your emotion instead of your message. If you feel stressed, paus a moment and take a three or four deep breath to calm yourself.

Own your experience. Avoid blaming anyone by continuing to use I statements: "I feel... I found... I am confused..." Don't look for other's approval of what you're saying. You are responsible for how you feel and your feelings merit respect.

Wait for an answer. It takes a few moments for people to respond to assertive communication. Give them time to think. Be comfortable with a few seconds of quiet. Wait. You'll receive more genuine, better quality answers.

When you apply these techniques, the recipient probably won't feel like he's being attacked. Your objection or concern is likely to be favorably and quickly resolved.

Resolve differences

Sometimes individuals are unwilling to agree to a decision and you're not sure what the problem is. For example, if someone appears to be attempting to prevent you from communicating or is otherwise frustrating group process, you need to resolve the situation. If you don't deal with issues on the spot, you'll have to deal with them later. So make a decision to do something, even if it means agreeing to resolve the issue later.

If you harbor resentment because someone hurts your feelings, you'll only cause ill feelings and damage your self-esteem. Don't give free rent in your head to someone who's bothered you. Avoiding being negative takes practice. If you're unable to resolve the issue with another person, then you need to forgive. Holding onto anger and resentment not only isn't fun, it's like drinking poison and expecting the other person to die.

List two ways to resolve differences when someone refuses to agree to a decision.

There are different ways you might respond:

Delay addressing the problem. Put the problem on hold. "John, I understand you have objections. We don't have the information needed to resolve your concerns now. Would you agree to put them on the back burner until 4:00? We'll work on getting answers then."

Empathize with them. Effective leaders show empathy and compassion for others. "John, I felt the same way when I started. I found out as I learned about the problem that there are answers to resolving this. Are you willing to set them aside for now with the understanding we'll circle back later to see if your issues have been resolved?"

Resolve it. If the group is willing and you have the time, ask clarifying questions to determine the underlying issue holding the individual back. For example, "What do you need to agree to move forward?" Be careful, because you're putting someone on the spot in front of the entire group. You don't want to back them into a corner or embarrass them.

Use body language

No matter how interesting the subject, nor how well prepared you may be, you aren't communicating successfully unless your learners learn—that is, they absorb what you're presenting.

List two ways to use body language to improve communication.

You want to engage your audience visually as well as by the force of your words, and spontaneous, coordinated body action express your enthusiasm and feeling for your subject.

Stand near the learners. If you're interacting with a reasonably sized group of 30 or less, walk around and stand near the learners from time to time. Be personal. Look at them in the eye. This is also an effective technique to pinch off distracting side-talk if you do it in a friendly manner.

Talk enthusiastically. Raise your voice and vary your pitch. Walk animatedly. Ask questions. Pause 5 or more seconds and wait for answers. Move around, using forceful gestures, and actively engaging participants. Look for those who like to hang back and purposefully involve them.

Lean in. Lean forward, pay attention, look at the learners, and ask questions that stimulate discussion.

Keep your body language in sync. Usabe body language deliberately. If you're saying one thing and your body is saying another, silent little alarm bells are ringing in your listener's mind. Keep your body language aligned with what you're communicating.

If you stand still while talking, it suggests to the listener that you don't have any feelings or convictions about your subject, or that you're sick or afraid.

Project ideas

List three ways to project your ideas to improve communication.

Learners respond to your:

Voice quality. Project a confident attitude. Speak clearly, use good diction, take your time, and speak loudly enough so everyone hears you.

Your attitude. Through the skillful use of your voice, your body, and your "presence"—sometimes called plain old enthusiasm—project your ideas and feelings to the learners in a memorable and pleasant way. In other words, the learning outcomes of your efforts depend, in good part, on your manner and style.

Your learners don't know the real you, only who you appear to be. Learners are attracted to people who radiate warmth, good humor, confidence, and pleasure at assisting others. Projecting a confident attitude is something leaders learn to do—and a useful technique for you as a Manager of Learning. Your behavior as a Manager of Learning is more important than what you say.

People don't care how much you know until they know how much you care.

Love the people under your stewardship.

If you act timid, fearful, or unprepared, learners sense this. Forced bluster can't conceal it. If you're winging it, don't apologize. You won't gain participants' sympathy or patience and you won't improve your presentation. Be confident, act enthusiastic, and give it your best shot. A positive attitude always helps people learn.

Eye contact. You "reach" others through your eyes, and a listener feels gratified that the speaker is actually looking at him—but look also at your audience for reactions. The raised eyebrow, the puzzled expression, should warn you to clarify your position or settle any misunderstanding immediately. Be sensitive to how the learners are receiving your communication. You would answer a spoken question—answer the unspoken ones too!

Coordinate your voice and body. When you have something to say, you want to say it with your whole being. "Suit the action to the word, and the word to the action" would be a good rule—we don't nod our head while saying "no!" nor shake our heads while saying "yes!" (Try it—it's confusing even to the one doing it.) Your gestures ought to arise from a normal, spontaneous desire to clarify or give emphasis. Your gestures should not call attention to themselves, but to your ideas—whatever you want people to learn or to feel.

List two examples of how body language varies between different cultures.

Body language varies between cultures. For example:

Head nodding. In the United States and Europe, shaking the head from side to side indicates "no," while in the India it means "yes".

Eye contact. In the United States, direct eye contact as an expression of honesty. But in many Asian cultures, looking directly at someone's eyes is seen as rude or aggressive.

Wave. In the United States, individuals say goodbye by holding their flat palm upward and waving it from side to side. But to many Europeans, this gesture simply means "no."

Using your voice

List four ways to use your voice effectively when communicating.

Use the varying qualities of your voice to enhance your delivery.

Pitch. A "good" voice has an interesting range of pitch. Start sentences on a pitch high enough to permit you to lower it for contrast, but low enough that you can raise it for contrast, also. Use the whole range of your voice by thinking—or feeling—what you're saying at that instant—not what you're going to say next.

Rate. Don't speak so slowly that the learners jump ahead of you or drift away or so rapidly that they're worn out keeping up. As with walking, variety is the key to interest—pauses permit appreciation. Use pauses as punctuation marks in speech—they're attention-getters. Don't panic at a few seconds of silence—it may take a few seconds for an idea to be absorbed.

Volume. If possible, check out in advance how much volume you must use to reach the farthest learner. Depending on the circumstances, you can ask, especially if someone looks quizzical or appears to be straining to hear. Don't forget that many bodies in a room tend to absorb noise and you may have to talk louder than you expect. However, most people aren't impressed with volume alone, and actors know the value of dropping their voices until the listeners participate by listening intently. Again, variety...!

Articulate. You must be instantly intelligible to everyone in your audience. Muffled and indistinct words suggest fuzzy thinking or mental slovenliness to some. Laziness is the curse—lazy lips, lazy jaws, and lazy tongues. Cleaning up casual speech habits that creep into your presentations takes work. If you have a habit of saying "uh", "uhm", or "you know", learn to pause and take a breath instead.

It's a good idea to start presenting to and interacting with small groups, where conversational custom permits you to "eye-ball" reactions and recognize instant demands for clarity.

But you don't have the visual option when presenting to a large group. Simply put, you need to rehearse. Once on the speaking platform, take time to speak clearly. If you're using a sound system or other technology, always "check your tech!"

Avoid buzz words

List three disadvantages of using acronyms.

Using acronyms is common when texting, but they are a problem when presenting new information to learners.

Don't abuse acronyms. When you form a new word from the initial letters or phrases of a group of words, you may create problems. Acronyms create a "we/they" mentality: those who belong, those who don't. Abbreviations and jargon alienate people who are new to your program.

Acronyms are duplicated. The same acronym exists in many different trades and fields but mean entirely different things. Or they may have an unintended and negative meaning you're unaware of. In 2003, the Coalition Provisional Authority began planning for a new Iraqi armed forces. They named it the New Iraqi Corps, or NIC. However, in Arabic "nic" is a colorful synonym for sex. The coalition renamed the force to the New Iraqi Army.

Acronyms are a crutch. Have you ever picked up a publication and found an often-used expression or jargon that is never, ever defined? While acronyms are an easy way to shorten laborious, repeated phrases, they also turn people off and exclude non-members.

When you abuse acronyms, you're unwittingly leading English teachers everywhere to join AAAAA, the American Association Against Acronym Abuse.

List one advantage of using acronyms.

Well-known acronyms. Acronyms are helpful when you're referring to well-known usages, like *scuba* or *laser*. (Self-Contained Underwater Breathing Apparatus. Light Amplification by Stimulated Emission of Radiation. You did know those were originally acronyms, didn't you?) Abbreviations and acronyms came into usage as a convenience for writers long before computers existed. Now that everything is written on a computer, acronyms are less necessary.

First time use. If you want to use acronyms, the first time you use one that isn't already widely accepted in common society, spell the phrase out fully and follow that with its abbreviation or acronym. After that, use the short form. For example, depending on the context, TNT might stand for Tuner Network Television or the explosive trinitrotoluene. So you might need to spell it out the first time.

But it's not necessary to give the meaning of FBI in everyday usage. (And if you always explain to your friends what IDK means, you can be sure they are ROFL.) An acronym is not the same as an abbreviation formed from the first letter(s) of words in a phrase. These letters are pronounced individually and do not become a new pronounceable word. For example: IBM (International Business Machine) and NCR (National Cash Register).

Abbreviations and acronyms are stimulating and helpful as a mnemonic device. The following are good examples as long as they aren't abused.

IEDAS (Introduction, Explanation, Demonstration, Application, Summary)

KISS (Keep it Simple Sweetheart)

KISMIF (Keep It Simple, Make It Fun)

Give feedback

Confirmation. Feedback is a way for you to verify that you heard communication accurately. It closes the communication "loop." Reflective listening is a form of giving feedback. For added information, see *Use reflective listening* on page 39.

Correction. It's also a way to communicate issues that you may see in another person or group. Feedback helps people keep behavior "on target" and in line with current goals.

List three characteristics of effective corrective feedback.

Characteristics of effective feedback include:

Descriptive rather than evaluative. Use neutral, objective language to describe what you observe. This helps the individual to listen and lessens their natural tendency to react defensively.

Specific rather than general. Specific feedback is descriptive and precise. A general statement isn't informative. For example, if you are told that your behavior was "dominating" a group or situation, you're left wondering exactly that means.

Considers the receiver's needs. Feedback is destructive when it serves only your needs and fails to consider the needs of the person on the receiving end.

Focused on changeable behavior. Frustration is only increased when a person is reminded of a shortcoming over which he has no control (a lisp, for example).

Solicited, rather than imposed. Feedback is most useful at the earliest opportunity after the given behavior, depending, of course, on the person's readiness to hear it and support available from others.

Verified to insure clear communication. One way of doing this is to have the receiver repeat back what was said to see if it corresponds to what the sender had in mind.

Validated for accuracy. When you give feedback, both the giver and receiver need an opportunity to check its accuracy. It may be useful to verify if anyone else feels the same way.

Uses "I-statements". By avoiding using "you", you can avoid putting the other person on the defensive. Using "I" keeps your comments on the side of opinion, not fact, and allows for discussion.

Feedback then, is a way of giving help. It's a corrective mechanism for people who want to match behavior to intentions.

Example. "A few minutes ago, when we were trying to make a decision, you were talking very loudly. I felt your tone sounded negative. I got the impression you weren't listening to what others said. I was afraid if I didn't accept your arguments, you would attack me."

Remember names

One of the most important behaviors that improves your relationship with your team members is to remember their names. When you know and use people's names, they feel connected with you. They know you care and are interested in them.

Successful leaders use a combination of techniques to remember people's names.

Repeat the person's name. Concentrate and repeat the person's names several times in the next few moments. Use it a few times aloud and repeat in silently to yourself.

For example, if the person's name is Diego, you might say, "Diego, it's great to meet you. Do you live around here Diego?"

Ask how to spell and pronounce it. Unless the spelling of both their first and last name is blindingly obvious, ask the individual to spell their name. If you are the least bit unsure about how to pronounce it correctly, ask them to say it for you. They'll appreciate that you care enough to ask, and you'll have an easier time remembering it. There are few *faux pas* more embarrassing than confidently greeting someone and getting their name wrong.

If you're introduced to Diego Zigarra, you might say, "Diego Zigarra—I don't think I've ever met someone with that last name? How do you spell it? Am I pronouncing it correctly?"

Associate it. If time permits, ask the person a few questions. Use the acronym FOR to learn about their Family, Occupation, and Recreation. As a teen, they may or may not have a job, but questions about these areas are the beginning of a relationship. When you hear something distinctive about the person, associate the person's name with that characteristic. If you don't have time to ask questions, associate their name with a distinctive physical characteristic.

For example, you might ask Diego if he plays sports, and he replies that he plays "futbol." So you repeat to yourself several times, "Diego Soccer Zigarra."

Take notes. Once you walk away, take notes about the person you met. Whip out your ever-handy leader's notebook and write down their name, where you met them, the date, and any other information that'll jog your memory later on.

Get a picture. If appropriate, take a selfie with them! People feel complimented when you want to remember them. Pictures make a big difference in remembering someone the next time you see them.

If you know beforehand that you might see someone you met before, take a few minutes and review your contact list, notes, and pictures from the last time you were there.

Give information

When giving information it's a good idea to use as many of the five senses. It isn't always appropriate to use all the senses, but if they contribute to communication, find ways to use as many as possible.

Use the five senses

Name the five senses and demonstrate how to use at least three of the five senses to transmit information.

Use the five senses to effectively communicate different types of information.

Imagine you have a friend who lives in a rural cabin on a farm in another part of the country. You visited him two summers ago. He calls you and tells you, "It's a nice day here." Would you know what he means?

Hearing. We rely on hearing extensively to receive information. Your friend told you it's a nice day where he is. But you want to know more. You've been to that place, but it's been a long time. You ask, "How nice a day is it?" Your friend replies, "Well, the birds are chirping and I can hear the bees in the trees. I can also hear the waterfall in the creek. The wind is rustling the leaves in the orchard."

Sight. Along with hearing, we rely on vision for most of the information we receive. You ask your friend, "What does the day look like?" He says, "Oh, you should be here. The sun is shining. There's a few puffy clouds in the sky. The apple trees in the orchard are loaded with beautiful, white blossoms."

Smell. After hearing and sight, we receive a large portion of information through our nose. Our most powerful memories are often associated with smell. Your friend says, "Do you remember the smell of the trees in bloom?" And suddenly you do, and you smile. "Well," your friend says, "if you're out front, you can't smell the blossoms today because the septic tank is overflowing."

Touch. We receive information through touch. You ask your friend, "What's it like out back by that big rock we liked to sit on?" He replies, "I'm lying on it now. It's real warm from the sun. If I could throw a pad on it now I'd be asleep in two minutes." You sigh, wishing you were with him right this second.

Taste. We also picked information from taste. Your friend says, "And that old lemon tree is still producing. I a half-dozen lemons earlier today. There's nothing like a tall glass of home-made lemonade on a hot day."

Use multiple senses. Beginning with, "It's a nice day," now you know the birds are chirping. You hear the noisy waterfall and the wind is rustling the trees. (Hearing) The sun is shining. There's not a cloud in the sky. The trees are a full of white blossoms. (Vision) You remember well the smell of the apple trees blossoming—and you can't forget the stink of the septic tank. (Smell!) Out back, the big, flat, smooth rock makes a great spot to rest. (Touch) And fresh lemonade can't be beat. (Taste) Now you know how nice a day it is!

So it's effective to use as many senses as possible when communicating with others.

Express yourself clearly

List four techniques for giving information clearly.

There are a number of techniques you can use to give information clearly. When giving information, remember to:

Speak and write to be understood. As a leader, you want to give information in an appropriate tone and manner. Speak or write succinctly and clearly without being bossy. If you give instructions during the job, keep it low key. Tell your team member the minimum they need to know. You want to encourage individual initiative and let people make significant contributions. They can't do that if you're watching over them like a hawk.

Speak clearly. The average rate of speaking for most Americans is from about 120 to 150 words per minute. You may need to vary your rate depending on your audience. Enunciate your words and talk in a way your audience understands. Make sure everyone hears you. While the information is probably familiar to you, the listener may be hearing it for the first time. Make sure you're speaking loud enough so the last person in the furthest seat hears you.

Use language that everyone understands. Avoid jargon and acronyms that may not be familiar with. Use language, ideas, and concepts the learner understands and relates to.

Vary your tone and pace. Keep your voice and the words you use interesting. Vary your intensity and tone depending on what you're communicating. If you're engaging the learners for longer than a few minutes, structure your presentation to build energy and enthusiasm among participants.

Generalize and be specific. Your goal is to assist the learners in moving from what they already know to what you want them to learn. Provide examples of generalizations that the learner relates to. Add specific examples that amplify your ideas.

Use visuals. Use charts, maps, and diagrams. Remember that people vary in how they best take in information. Selected people are oriented towards verbal language, others towards the written word, and many learn visually. Use simple charts and diagrams. If you can't communicate something simply, you probably haven't thought it through.

Eyeball the listener. If you're leading a group discussion, can you see everyone? Are they looking at you? If learners are hiding behind others, ask them to move. If possible, arrange them in a semi-circle so they are able to see each other. This encourages cross-communication and sharing ideas. If your audience is so far away you don't know if they're looking at you, observe their posture and the tilt of their head.

Encourage two-way flow. Ask the learners to answer questions and invite them to ask you questions. If you ask a question and if at first no one has an answer, take a moment and wait. Don't feel uncomfortable because no one is answering. This is a potent moment. You may have uncovered a gap in their knowledge that needs filling.

Verify if they understood your question, and then begin adding to what they know to close the gap for them. When they ask you questions, respond helpfully and in a friendly manner. Don't pass judgment on the question or the questioner.

Build others up

A little known leadership communication tool is to edify others, including family, friends, and team members. Your goal is to build others up, "to provide moral, intellectual, or spiritual instruction." An archaic use of the word is to "build [up] or establish," and this is a usage that's coming back into favor. List one way to edify or lift others up.

To edify others:

Praise them publicly. For example, suppose John put in extra hours to make sure a goal was completed. If you tell team members how much you appreciate John's effort, you show loyalty, faithfulness, appreciation, love, respect, and consideration. Without thumping your own chest, John appreciates and gains respect for you.

Raise their expectations. Edify others every day. It's natural to tell someone what they did wrong: "Dave, the scrambled eggs are cooked hard!" Instead, say, "I know you're capable of doing a good job when you apply yourself to it."

The person listening thinks better of himself while realizing they could have done a better job. And they respect your benevolent attitude. As a leader, edifying others is an act of service. It's a win/win for everyone.

Use reflective listening

Define two steps of reflective listening.

Reflective listening means to:

Repeat back. Reflecting communication means mirroring what you heard. It's not necessary to repeat what the person said word-for-word. It's usually enough to repeat the key words or the key ideas.

Obtain confirmation. Ask for verbal confirmation that what you repeated back agrees with what they said.

Reflect what you heard. Reflecting back confirms with the other person that you heard them accurately. You're checking with the sender for confirmation of your understanding. Reflecting helps to confirm that you understand the other person's thoughts and emotions. Having received confirmation that you understand, it allows the other person to continue.

When you listen to someone, it's the most profound act of human respect. —William Ury

List three characteristics of reflective listening.

To be effective, reflective listening is:

Non-judgmental. Your feedback doesn't evaluate the individual's statements or emotions. This simply lets him know that you've heard him and helps build trust that you aren't judging him for how he feels.

Concise. You restate and summarize what you heard the person say. You use the individual's language as much as possible. If you hear emotion in their voice, you may reflect that back too by describing the nature and intensity of his feelings. By reflecting his emotions, you're also validating that his feelings are genuine. Now he knows that you have an objective perception of what he is saying and feeling.

Accurate. You correctly reflect the content of what the speaker said. If you're wrong, then correct your notes.

Example: The learner says, "My teacher doesn't listen to me. When I try to ask a question, he passes me up and answers someone else's question." You reflect back, "You're frustrated. Your teacher is ignoring you and you're not getting the information you need."

Let people know you're listening

List four behaviors that let people know that you're listening.

There are at least four ways to encourage others to talk to you.

Give the individual your undivided attention. Stop whatever you're doing. Invite the person to sit down. If appropriate, find a location where you can talk privately.

Maintain eye contact. Don't stare him down, but look directly at him and show your interest.

Use the individual's name. People feel important and appreciated when you use their name.

Smile, relax, and be friendly. Make him feel that you're eager to hear what he has to say.

Remove communication barriers

List five behaviors that block effective communication.

Negative attitudes and motivation. Participants' motivation affects their attitude. The listener may perceive that they already know the topic. They may feel it conflicts with other beliefs or information they previously acquired.

The person giving information may lack credibility or authority in the mind of the listener, causing them to discount any communication originating with that individual. The source of the lack of trust may be based on prior experience or it could be based on uninformed perceptions, including stereotypes.

Social or cultural differences. Individual's cultural or social backgrounds may influence communication. Words and their meaning may be misunderstood. Individual's beliefs and values may influence what they understand. For example, holding the thumb upward in most of Latin America means "OK", but is Islamic countries it's a rude sexual gesture.

Conflicting communication. If the listener is getting two different messages, the communication fails. People believe what they see, not what they hear. If a leader talks about the importance of setting the example, but interrupts you or is uses offensive language, they lose credibility.

Experience or bias. People build belief systems over time that affect what they like and dislike. The may associate one thing with another, and they judge the second based on the first. Their bias, hidden or obvious, affects the flow of information. **Example**: If an individual associates motorcycles with biker gangs, they may automatically be suspicious of anyone who rides a motorcycle. So they might be surprised to learn the rider is an attorney and the CVO Road Glide he owns cost more than $40,000.

Physical discomfort and distractions. The receiver isn't listening because other issues are on his or her mind, such as, physical discomfort, personal problems, or other immediate ideas. These issues prevent learners from paying attention to long-range ideas.

Get information

List the two senses used most often to receive information.

There are two primary senses we use to receive information.

Through our ears. Orally from another person.

Through our eyes. Through writing and illustrations.

Information we receive varies in complexity. It might be utterly simple, for example:

"Meet me at the school gym at 7:00 sharp Wednesday night."

Or it might be extremely complex:

"From the start, go due north 122 feet to the maple tree. Walk back the direction you came 10 feet. Go 145 degrees at 3 miles per hour for 2 minutes. Stop at the red cedar tree. Turn 25 degrees south..."

When you don't communicate information accurately, two problems may arise:

- Facts are forgotten.
- Facts are distorted.

This may happen for two reasons:

- The individual sending the information isn't clear, or
- The person receiving the information fails to accurately retain the communication.

Control communication

List two factors you control when giving information.

As a sender, you control:

What you say. What you say is the content of the message.

How you say it. How you say something includes verbal and non-verbal cues to the content, including the tone, method, body language, and so forth.

List two ways a recipient controls the information they receive.

As a recipient of information, you control what you hear.

Listen and watch. The message you receive is affected by verbal and non-verbal cues, and your ability to understand the cues. These may or may not be what the sender intended.

Mirror what you heard. Mirror what you thought you heard back to the sender. To be sure that the message sent was the message received, verbally repeat back to the sender the information you believe you received. This doesn't mean to parrot back exactly what you heard. It means to paraphrase in your own words what you understood, including the emotions.

I know you think you understand what you thought I said but I'm not sure you realize that what you heard is not what I meant. –Alan Greenspan

Retrieve information

As you receive information, use specific techniques to improve your ability to accurately recall what you heard.

List five ways to remember and retrieve information so that it isn't forgotten or distorted.

There are a few ways to improve how you remember information.

Memorization

Memorization is only useful for brief tidbits of information that you want to retrieve soon afterward. Memories are usually quickly vaporized by either of two factors:

Quantity. There's always too much to remember. That's why so many people make the mistake of using the same password over and over again.

Time. As time passes, it's harder to accurately remember what you heard. Have you ever asked someone a question, gotten an answer, and after walking away did an about face and asked the question again? Ok, maybe that only applies to people over 40.

Unless you have that rare gift of a photographic memory, memorizing information rarely works. There are too many chances for remembering information inaccurately.

Association

Think 'Lean Gene.' When you associate one piece of information with another, it is easier to remember. Suppose you're introduced to Gene. You notice he's skinny, so you think, "Lean Gene."

L for Port. Or maybe you're taking sailing lessons for the first time. Knowing the correct names for each side of the boat is critical, so you say to yourself, "Left for port—both have four letters and end in 'T'. (If you're having a bad day and don't remember which one is your left hand, here's a hint: hold out both hands and make an "L" with your thumb and forefinger. The correctly shaped L is on your left hand. See how simple it is?)

The biggest challenge using association is remembering the association.

Repetition

Repeating information has two key advantages.

Retention. Repeating information helps you retain what you heard. For example, to remember Gene's name, use it several times in the first few minutes after you're introduced. Then repeat it to yourself several times.

Understanding. Repeating information helps you check your understanding. This is sometimes called active listening.

But repeating information is a weak retrieval system. You can't easily remember lots of information over a long period of time.

- Reduces the chances you distort the meaning of what you heard
- Helps you remember the information.
- Helps you clarify and verify!

Recording

Sure, recording is the most accurate way to retain information, but it's not necessarily the easiest way to retrieve something later on. It's always a good idea to supplement your notes with a recording. But that assumes you're actually going to take the time to listen to the recording.

Listening to a recording is time-intensive, so only record important discussions and talks, the type that motivate you to want to listen to them again.

Take notes

If you want to retain what you're hearing, note taking is the best method to retrieve information. If you don't take notes, what you're saying is that what you're hearing isn't worth remembering. However, your notes are only as good as your note-taking system.

The palest ink is better than the best memory. –Chinese proverb

Get a notebook. Notes scribbled on loose scraps of paper are easily lost. Remember that important piece of information in your wallet or purse that you never found? Keep notes in a sturdy notebook. As a leader, you always want a notebook and pen handy.

Use an app. If you're using an app, choose one that recognizes handwriting so you can write on the screen, unless you can keyboard quickly with your thumbs. Choose an app that allows you to export your notes, that's backed up to the cloud. Then sync your notes and share them as needed.

List three techniques for taking notes.

Techniques for taking notes include:

Write down key words. Write down important instructions, concepts, issues, directions, comments. Answer main questions like who, what, where, when, why and how. Use key words and partial sentences. Abbreviate and use acronyms. Write or print clearly, so you can read it and make sense of it later on.

Listen for the main points. Good speakers usually tip you off by saying words like, "There are three major reasons why.... The first is..."

Ask the speaker to repeat. "Ms. Jones, I am not sure I caught the last point. Would you please state it again?

Visualize. If you're visually oriented, draw a sketch, map, or diagram. Charts and pictures help you remember information. Draw diagrams to illustrate relationships. Use cloud charts to organize your thoughts. Draw flow charts to indicate process. Annotate your pictures with labels and symbols you understand.

Outline. Use outline style.

1. Let the outline show the relation of ideas. Here is a standard outline pattern:
   a. Capital letters are subheads under Roman numerals.
      i. Arabic numerals are subheads under capitals.
         1. Small letters are subheads under Arabic numerals.

Be succinct. Don't write full statements. On the other hand, don't be so sketchy that it doesn't mean anything later. Brief, accurate, notes are better than lengthy, confused ones.

Review your notes

Add action steps. Within 24 hours, before your notes are cold, read them and make sure you understand what you wrote. Add other information as needed. Spend a few profitable minutes fixing the main points of the discussion in your mind and write down what you intend to do about it. One technique that works is to mark key passages with numbers or letters to indicate a next step. For example, use *A* to indicate *Action* and *F* to indicate *File*.

Communicate during meetings

Vital communication takes place during meetings. Use meetings to sync everyone's work, to identify and resolve roadblocks, to celebrate progress and success, and to plan the next steps. To be sure information is accurately communicated and retained, write down key points during the meeting.

Use meetings wisely

As a leader, you're in charge of meetings. Your goal is to keep meetings brief, specific, and action-oriented. Meetings are incredibly important, but they can be truly bad. Only have a meeting if it has a specific purpose.

Designate a decision-maker. If no one is responsible, nothing gets done.

Distribute an agenda beforehand. Prepare a short summary or agenda of what the meeting is about and send it to participants a day or two before the meeting is held. This helps keep everyone focused.

Keep meetings small. Just like building a team, an effective meeting is limited to eight people. Too many participants cause meetings to go over-long and dilute responsibility, allowing individuals to hang back, figuring that someone else will do it.

Set a time limit. Open-ended meetings are a nightmare. Set times to begin and end the meeting and stick to those times. You gain participant's respect when you start on time and end on time. If you can't complete your agenda, agree on another meeting later on.

Take breaks. If your meeting includes several learning sessions that take several hours, schedule breaks. The mind can only take in what the seat can tolerate!

Keep notes. To be sure information is accurately communicated and retained, the decision-maker asks someone to take notes. This person might only be a note-taker, but may also be the facilitator. Your goal isn't to transcribe everything that was said, but to capture the key points and the specific commitments made. For related information about taking notes, see *Use flip charts effectively* on page 48.

Facilitate group progress

Use a facilitator. A facilitator is a specialized role who helps the group to be open and genuine. A facilitator produces better quality ideas and increase group participation. A facilitator relieves you of the multiple roles of group process watch dog, timekeeper, and content input processor. The facilitator's most important role is channeling and focusing group communication.

A good facilitator isn't wedded to a particular outcome but to the group's success. The facilitator's role is distinctive.

- He doesn't contribute his own ideas, but remains neutral.
- He works with everyone until the group has reached agreement.
- He focuses the energy of the group on the task as needed.
- He defends group members from attack.

He may make process suggestions, e.g., "The time we contracted for this item is nearly up...shall we conclude discussion or do you want to contract for additional time?"

Set ground rules

The facilitator isn't the boss of anyone. He acts as the group's "traffic cop," keeping group process flowing during meetings. As prevention, the facilitator:

- Sets ground rules, defines roles.
- Gets agreement on process.
- Gets agreement on content/outcome.
- Stays neutral, out of content areas.
- Is positive, has a win/win attitude.
- Suggests process as needed.
- Educates the group to process procedures.
- Gets permission to enforce process agreements.

- Gets the group to take responsibility for its actions.

- Builds the agenda.

- Secures ownership by the group of the agenda.

- Sets up the meeting location.

Keep the group on track

List three ways a leader helps the group succeed during meetings.

During a meeting, a facilitator employs different strategies to keep the group on track:

- Boomerang the question or concern back to the group when they should answer it: "How does the rest of the group feel about this?"

- Maintain/regain focus: "What's the real issue here?"

- Play dumb: "Can someone tell me what's going on?"

- Say what's going on when destructive behavior occurs.

- Check for agreement: "OK?"

- Avoid process battles; there is more than one way.

- Enforce process agreements: "Sorry, your time is up."

- Encourage all members' participation.

- Use the group memory.

- Don't talk too much.

- Accept/legitimize, deal with, or defer.

- Don't be defensive; let the group decide what's correct or not.

- Use body language positively.

Use flip charts effectively

You can use flip charts for all kinds of presentations during meetings and learning sessions. Using flip charts effectively is an important and effective skill. Flip charts have a bunch of advantages for you as a Manager of Learning.

Choose a low-tech solution

A few people don't believe they've participated in a training session or meeting unless they have been subjected to at least one high-tech, animated, slide presentation. Unfortunately, some trainers think this way too.

Use display devices sparingly. Depending on their purpose, projectors can be an effective way to communicate information. Presentation slides are common in the business world and in classrooms. But they assume that the participants all know nothing. They are a one-way tool—there's no allowance for feedback on screen. Printing and sharing slides is time-consuming and photocopying them is expensive. And if you're presenting learning activities outdoors, most trees don't come with built-in electrical outlets.

Avoid white or chalk boards. White boards and chalk boards are only useful if you're meeting indoors. You can't easily retain what you write on these boards, unless you transcribe them, a time-consuming task.

And since you're developing a hands-on program, one of your goals is to be outdoors whenever possible. If you use a white board indoors and a flip chart outdoors, you may struggle when making the switch and lose credibility with your learners. It's always a good idea to use the same presentation methods wherever you are so that you are experienced, confident, and prepared.

Adapt to the circumstances. Flip charts are inexpensive, simple to make, and portable. If your learners are seated at a table or on chairs, you only need a flip chart paper and a stand. If you're leading a discussion with a small group of eight or less, allowing you to get up close and personal, you can make your presentation ultra-portable. Just use a large artist's sketch pad with a stiff cardboard backing.

Flip chart guidelines

Before putting marker to paper, remember:

Use thick paper. You don't want your markers to bleed through onto the paper behind.

Use dark colors. Use color or high-lighters for variety and impact, not for "beauty." Use a maximum of 3 colors, more often, only 2. Use colors that are easily read from a distance. Don't use highlighters. Too much color distracts from the content.

Print. Don't use cursive, even if you know what that is.

Write for "back row" visibility. Use block letters and a square, medium marker. Make letters tall enough to read at a distance:

10 ft. — 1/2 in.	20 ft. — 3/4 in.
30 ft. — 1 in.	40 ft. — 1 1/2 in.

Reveal one idea at a time. Or start with blank pages and ask open-ended question to solicit group input; let the learners construct the chart.

Record group members' input. Have a group member transcribe the chart paper for reproduction and later distribution.

Use understandable graphics. Make your symbols, pictures, and diagrams obvious and simple.

Reveal your ideas deliberately. Choose when you want to reveal your ideas; conceal them after you no longer need them. These are the real advantages of flip charts.

Plan your flip charts

List three reasons to prepare flip charts in advance.

To be an effective Manager of Learning, prepare your flip charts in advance.

Plan your pages. Write down your flip chart notes on binder paper first. Keep your content simple and short.

Choose your location. Figure how and where you want to place the flip chart. For a full-size flip chart, use an easel. Tip: Duct tape is your friend! Tape the legs to the floor and the flip chart to the easel. If you're going ultra-portable, a table top easel might work.

Outline your content. Make little mistakes first. Use a pencil to outline your content in the margins of the flip chart. This steers your discussion and keeps you on track.

Keeps ideas fluid. Don't let your flip chart notes straitjacket your discussion or become a crutch for you to hobble through your allotted time. If someone brings up new or interesting ideas, you always have room to add them. If you finally found a well-chosen word doesn't mean it's sacred—the learners may come up with one they like better. Whatever turns them on...that's the idea!

Find your spot. Flip charts are unruly in winds, tear instead of turn, topple instead of tear, and attack the unwary and innocent. Lighting and visibility are critical. Find a good spot to place your flip chart stand. Use at least a half roll of duct tape to make sure it doesn't move.

Keep it simple sweetheart. Use only key words. Expose one idea at a time. Help learners focus on what's most important. People may be so busy taking notes that they miss the meat of your presentation. Or you miss out because they might have had something valuable to contribute. If possible, give participants an outline of your flip chart in advance so they can pay full attention. Then encourage them to take notes using your outline.

List two advantages of using flip charts during a meeting or discussion.

Use flip charts to:

Keep a record. Remove pages from the flip chart after you finish a topic and post them on the wall where everyone can view them. Or take pictures of the pages, or keep the pages and transcribe them later.

Stay honest. If you're taking notes of a group discussion, use a flip chart to record ideas accurately. Notes on a flip chart also guard against data overload. Use the flip chart to hold ideas so participants are able to focus on the issue and not what someone said.

Be cheap. Compared to a computer projector, paper flip charts are cheap. To save even more money, buy spools of suitable paper and roll your own flip charts.

Go low tech. Use flipcharts indoors or out. Roll it up and slip your flip chart under your arm. You're now an Instant Presenter. Take your roll any place you go. You're not stuck hauling around an awkward, bulky white board. You don't need to worry if the new learning activity location has an outlet nearby, or carry 1000 feet of extension cord, "just in case."

Improvise. Make a flipchart with the simplest of tools. Unlike that digital presentation, a flip chart is easily modified. As a manager of learner, you are concentrating on what the learner needs, not what you're presenting. A flip chart is an easy way to record and recognize learners' contributions and ideas.

Move forward. When everyone sees in big letters exactly what they've been doing, it adds to their sense of accomplishment. If someone arrives late or zones out, they can easily catch up with the group by referring to the pages from the flip chart that you've taped to the walls or hung from a line between a couple of nearby trees.

Participants own what they're learning by using language they understand.

Follow up. Make accountability and follow up easier; who does what is written down in full view of the entire group.

Resources of the Group

About Resources of the Group

The competency Resources of the Group is usually introduced as the group is becoming a team. Presenting this competency helps to improve group morale and team spirit.

This competency describes methods that help leaders learn about group members' resources or their attitude, skills, and knowledge. It enhances the accidental, serendipitous "getting to know you" process that takes place in groups.

It provides an informal but recognized stage when these forming steps can be intentionally managed. The formal process increases the intensity of the exchanges, promoting honesty and trust. It accelerates the rate at which the group begins to coalesce and develop commitment to a common purpose. Greater productivity and success are the result.

To build the group's cohesiveness, give them challenges that require them to work together. Introduce activities that force the individuals in the group to become acquainted with one another's skills, knowledge, and attitudes. Your goal is to challenge the individuals and the group in such a way that they need to rely on each other.

Objectives

When you complete presenting the content in this chapter, learners are able to:

- Define a resource.
- Define the difference between attitudes, skills and knowledge.
- List two reasons you need to know group member's attitudes, skills and knowledge.
- List two ways a group learns about the resources of its members.
- List three characteristics of human resources.
- Define two characteristics of physical resources.
- List one person in a group who needs to know the entire group's resources
- State the biggest reason that more people don't achieve their dreams.
- List the most important human resource a leader relies on.
- List one reason autocratic or authoritarian organizations don't tend to prosper.
- Define who's responsible for providing direction and leadership within a group.
- List two reasons leadership belongs to the group and not one individual.

Imagine

Your little idea a few weeks ago to help kids learn to camp has suddenly gotten big. The local college is putting on a community fair and has invited your group. They want to get the word out about Kamping for Kids.

The local newspaper learned about your group from the college. They want to write an article. Time is short – the newspaper wants to have the article ready in 10 days. The reporter says they'll also video record the interview.

Your team is a little nervous. The simple idea you had to go camping and have fun is turning serious. The enthusiastic volleyball team captain likes the idea of giving kids a fun time. The community fair is a great chance to let people know what you are planning. You hope to recruit more youth to assist with the camping trip. If the video shoot goes well, you plan to post it to YouTube, Vimeo, and other sites.

Of course everyone wants to be interviewed by the reporter. But a few group members speak with an accent that is hard to understand. One member has taken drama classes; another is on the debate team.

While your group is excited, they are also a little disorganized. You want to let people know that you are serious about your interest. You decide to buy T-shirts or polo shirts for everyone to wear. Then you suddenly realize you need a logo for the shirts. All of this needs to happen in a few days.

Given the resources within your group, how will you complete all these tasks? Who's going to create a logo and order shirts for everyone? Where's the money going to come from? Based on their skills and experience, who will you choose to speak to the reporter?

Describe resources

Define a resource.

A resource is:

- Anything in the environment.
- Group attitudes, knowledge, and skills.

Define the difference between attitudes, knowledge, and skills.

Some differences between attitudes, knowledge, and skills are:

Attitude. Attitude is a way of thinking or feeling. Attitude influences your feelings, motivation, belief, and confidence.

Knowledge. The facts, truths, or principles you know. Knowledge controls what you do.

Skill. An ability or capacity that you've gained from purposeful, sustained, and systematic effort. Usually applies to complex activities involving cognitive skills (the brain), motor skills (the muscles), and interpersonal skills (people).

For example, while you may be excited about learning to play a violin (attitude), and you know the parts of a violin and even how to hold it (knowledge), you can't play a single note (skill). And no matter how long you take lessons, if you don't have the attitude required, you won't succeed.

If talent alone is enough, then why do you and I know highly talented people who are not highly successful? John Maxwell

To become successful in any endeavor, you need attitude, knowledge, *and* skills. But your attitude is most important.

Your attitude, not your aptitude, will determine your altitude.—Zig Zigler

List two reasons you need to know group member's attitudes, skills and knowledge.

Reasons it's important to learn group members' attitudes, skills and knowledge include:

Using the group's resources. As a leader, it's important to become familiar with your team members' knowledge, experience, strengths, skills, and abilities. These resources play a vital role in the team's success. Encouraging individuals to contribute their resources enables them to take a leadership role. When team members assume responsibility for the team's success, the team is more likely to achieve its goals.

Helping group members grow. Groups only grow when its individual members grow. You must know the team member's attitudes, skills and knowledge so you can develop plans that support individual growth. When members grow, they feel increased loyalty towards the group.

Building relationship. When you're familiar with group members, you can relate to members more effectively. Knowing about an individual's attitudes, skills and knowledge, and their related strengths and experiences, is a starting point for conversation. Conversation is a way to open up communication, and communication opens up possibilities for relationship.

Respond to challenges. You need to be able to respond to situations and challenges as they arise. You can't wait until the challenge arises to find out what skills a particular member has.

List two ways a group learns about the resources of its members.

Groups learn about the resources of its members at least two ways:

Informally. Any time a group first comes together, there's a process of "getting to know you" always takes place. Depending on, among other characteristics, members' age, experience, and cultural background, standard rituals of introduction take place, including questions like, "Where do you live? What school do you attend? What do you like to do? Where did you grow up? What do you do when you aren't working or in school?" From this conversation, group members develop an informal assessment of other group members' attitude and ability.

Formally. When a group is first given a task, members ask specific questions and find out who has the skills needed, or what resources exist within the group. However, an effective leader begins to develop a formal assessment of group resources right away. He is already knowledgeable about the group's goals. He asks questions to learn about group members' attitudes, skills and knowledge. He seeks to match group member's skills against the likely challenges the group faces.

Human resources

List three characteristics of human resources.

Human resources. We don't mean personality characteristics. People's resources include:

- Attitudes
- Skills
- Knowledge

Human resources are, for our purposes, inexhaustible. As leaders we primarily work through others; we assume that everyone's limits have not been reached, and that no one ever reaches their fullest potential.

A leader takes people where they want to go. A great leader takes people where they don't necessarily want to go, but ought to be. —Rosalynn Carter

Physical resources

Define two characteristics of physical resources.

Physical resources. This includes objects in the environment, like rope, poles, chairs, or pots and pans. Physical resources are, by our general definition, all inclusive. They include the tangible and intangible—the sun, trees, people, time, a knife—everything is a resource.

The environment around you. Physical resources are the tangible assets found in our environment. While physical assets may at first impression be useful only for a specific purpose, creative leaders improvise and find multiple ways to use what is available to them.

Resources are unlimited

Because a tangible resource isn't immediately available, you don't automatically stop moving forward.

Improvise! If specific physical resources aren't available, improvise! You figure out how to "make do" with the resources on hand. The only limit on our resources is often only our mind. All of us have the potential for moments to become James Bond as he whips off his shoe laces to save himself from certain death.

The ability to identify and utilize resources that no one else recognizes is a hallmark of a leader. Creativity, ingenuousness, and the ability to respond to dynamic, fluid situations are essential characteristics of the top-notch leader.

Identify group resources

List one person in a group who needs to know the entire group's resources.

Everyone. The entire team.

In a top-performing team, the leader *and* each team member are jointly responsible for knowing and making effective use of the group's resources. The group as a whole is a tremendous collection of knowledge, skills, and abilities. Your challenge as a leader is to get to know each individual and learn about their individual talents. Collectively, you can accomplish significantly more than any one person.

As a leader, look for new methods and ideas that support your team's goals. Because your team is closest to your opportunities or challenges, you have the most information and are usually best equipped to resolve it. To produce effective results, combine the new methods you find with your group's talents.

At the end of the 20th century, American business began to recognize that the most effective way to make decisions is to push responsibility for decision making to the lowest possible level.

Think out of the box

The human spirit's capacity for achievement and innovation is enormous. Yet few if any schools teach what it takes to be successful.

State the biggest reason that more people don't achieve their dreams.

Stinking thinking. The greatest limitation most people experience is our own limited thinking.

- We develop "mindsets" or ways of thinking that inhibit our ability to think outside the box.
- We tend to generalize too broadly, or think in black and white (either/or) terms.
- We sometimes live up to an impossible standard: "I should never make mistakes." "I'll never be as good as Leeann."
- We magnify mistakes out of proportion to their actual impact. Little obstacles become major roadblocks.

■ We fear the worst. After hearing a report of a shark attack in Australia, we are afraid to take a dip in Florida.

Stuck inside the box. Moving out of our own way is the greatest challenge many people face in their entire lives. Adults are often a collection of bad habits well-learned. We limit our access to all types of resources, ideas, talents, competencies, skills, knowledge and attitudes that contribute to success. Individuals carry these beliefs into their organization, which reflects their attitude. Now the institutions or organizations live inside a make-believe box of limitations.

The world as we have created it is a process of our thinking. It cannot be changed without changing our thinking. —Albert Einstein

Keep an open mind. We need to think "outside the box." Many leaders are increasingly aware of the need to think creatively. One of the most important resources we possess as individuals is an open mind and creative thinking.

People with a positive attitude are influenced by what does on within them. People with a negative attitude are influenced by what goes on around them. —Keith Harrell

Push decision-making down

For example, auto factory management employed analysts who would complete time-and-motion studies on how long it takes a factory worker to make a certain part, or the "best" configuration for an assembly line. The analysts made decisions for entire teams of people. The assembly line workers hated the time-and-motion "experts." The workers on the assembly line felt they were being treated as robots or cogs in the wheel, not individuals with brains.

Instead of restricting key information to higher levels of management, companies that are more successful are providing line employees with direct access to information that affects their work and productivity. The assembly line workers are empowered to use their own resources to solve production line problems, in cases resulting in vast increases in efficiency.

Create passion

List the most important human resource a leader relies on.

Involve the team. An effective leader helps the team develop a passion for the project by involving them emotionally and improving their attitude.

Everyone sees physical resources around them. Effective leaders learn to seek out the unseen resources, the team's values, commitment, and jointly held aspirations. Effective leaders rely on insight, inspiration, and foresight to find opportunities. He shows respect for team members and their contributions.

Tap their imagination. The effective leader also taps into people's imagination, encouraging them to apply innovative solutions. He creates loyalty by helping team members' meet their wants, needs, and desires. As he does all these, he helps members achieve their aspirations, builds increased loyalty, and a commitment from them to attain team and organizational goals.

Make individuals count

List one reason autocratic or authoritarian organizations don't tend to prosper.

Individuals don't count. In authoritarian environments, individual contributions aren't valued. A person's talents, abilities, and experience are often ignored.

For example, the quality of American automobiles suffered for years because, in part, individuals felt they had little impact on the effort to produce a quality product. When they spotted a defect, the assembly line workers were effectively disabled from contributing even their intelligence, for they had no means to stop the production line and correct the problem. Giving workers the ability to stop the assembly line when a defect was spotted immediately raised the quality of the finished product, while not significantly slowing production.

Draw on group resources

To be successful, tap into every member's resources.

Share responsibility. Suppose a factory team gathers to solve a quality control problem—a formed sheet of metal rattles in its place on an assembled product. Does the piece have to be redesigned from scratch? New holes machined? Extra mounting screws added? (What is the most cost-effective solution?)

The best solution may involve everyone—the designer, machinist, assembler, and manager—even the customer. Anyone left out—their knowledge, their resources—could make a huge difference in the quality of the decision and people's commitment to it. Diverse people have a variety of resources to contribute.

Know your team. If members of your team have ten different types of skills, how many of them do you personally need to be able to perform?

None.

You job is to help people work effectively and provide them with an environment in which they prosper.

Like the auto workers on an assembly line, do you need to possess the engineer's design capabilities, the machinist's knowledge of material tolerances, and the assembler's eye for ease of construction? No. Your role is to find someone who has the skills, knowledge, or abilities required and rely on him.

Empower your team. One leader who didn't have technical expertise but led a team that had a huge impact is Eric Doremus. In 1992, Honeywell's defense avionics division reorganized their organization into multifunctional teams. Division management selected individuals to become supervisors who could facilitate loyalty, communication and decision making. One of the supervisors chosen was Doremus, who had spent seven years in marketing and sales.

Doremus was charged with leading a 40-person team to develop a data storage system for Northrop Grumman's B-2 stealth bomber. Despite having no technical background, Doremus successfully led the group by fostering team loyalty and focusing their effort on the Air Force's needs. He saw his job as helping the team "feel as if they owned the project by getting whatever information, financial or otherwise, they needed. I knew that if we could all charge the hill together, we would be successful."

Delegate leadership

Define who's responsible for providing direction and leadership within a group.

Everyone. There isn't a single person on your team responsible for knowing the entire team's resources. Everyone is responsible.

You're not solely responsible for knowing everyone else's resources. It's a good idea for you to know as much as possible about all his team members. But the wise and secure leader is able to rely on group members to be familiar with each other's attitude, skills, and knowledge. As a skilled leader, you have enough self-esteem that you feel free to seek assistance from someone better than you are. You are confident and willing to delegate control of a situation to an individual with the ability to resolve it.

Since leadership is a property of the group, everyone is responsible for learning and sharing their individual and communal resources. When team members recognize that you value their contributions, their loyalty to their fellow team members and the organization grows. Team members are more confident about the ongoing success of their efforts when they know they have "depth in the outfield."

Share leadership

List two reasons leadership belongs to the group and not one individual.

If a group has ten members and one leader, how many members can the group rely on for leadership and direction? Eleven.

Leadership is a property of the group. Everyone has resources that benefit the group. Depending on the situation, one or more group members may possess the needed attitude, skills, and knowledge.

Everyone is involved. Sharing leadership has multiple benefits to the group and group members. When you ask individuals to contribute, they feel more involved and committed. When you properly motivate and recognize members for their contribution, they feel an increased loyalty to you and the group.

Drawing on the resources of the group helps build two- and three-deep leadership, building up redundancies within the organization so it functions effectively, especially in times of stress.

Needs and Characteristics of the Group

About Needs and Characteristics of the Group

Before you lead others, you must first understand them. Understand what drives people: their needs and characteristics. Only when you know and understand others are you in a position to lead them.

As you mature, your ability to understand others slowly grows, like ivy climbing a tree over many seasons. Without pruning, ivy chokes a tree and eventually kills it. Without direction and education, you gain the ability to understand others haphazardly, and you may not know what to do with the information you gain. Without understanding others' needs and characteristics, you may hurt them and yourself.

For adults who lead teens, they are responsible for helping them mature into leaders. It's their job to fertilize, prune, and shape—to counsel and mentor—them. They need to directly explore and encourage youth to discover their personality traits.

Teens are prone to fragment into homogeneous groups. While full of emerging strengths, they may be quick to judge other's weaknesses. As an effective leader, you recognize that every member has strengths and weaknesses and all can contribute to the group.

When any group forms, its members develop an informal assessment of other members' needs and characteristics. The leadership competency *Knowing the Needs and Characteristics of the Group* brings the process out of the closet.

The highest order of needs is something required for survival, like food and water. But individuals also need a comfortable chair to sit in or to go to the bathroom.

A characteristics or personality trait is what others see. It's a personal landmark others judge you by (sometimes accurately, sometimes not).

To build your team, it's your job as the leader to create an open, trusting environment where members of your group feel their needs are met and feel like they belong. You do this by developing and engaging your youth in learning activities and exercises designed to foster discovery and trust. Your goal is to create a place where everyone feels accepted and individual differences are valued. You want them to learn that individual differences contribute to an environment calculated to encourage growth.

To help a group evolve into a team, you must learn about individuals needs and support their growth. Knowing group members' needs and characteristics is an essential step. A group is merely a serendipitous gathering of individuals who may or may not have goals in common. They're unlikely to form a sustained relationship. A team is a cooperative, cohesive unit that has developed an ongoing relationship. They're working together to accomplish specific tasks and goals. For adults guiding teens, they want to help them acquire skills and become more effective leaders.

Objectives

When you complete presenting the content in this chapter, learners are able to:

- List at least six characteristics of values.
- List two reasons values are important to a leader.
- List two values that high-performing teams usually embrace.
- List two types of norms.
- Define the difference between a need and a want.
- List four needs common to everyone.
- List two reasons it's important for a leader to be able to identify his own needs.
- List four needs common to virtually everyone.

- Define motivation.

- List two characteristics of motivation.

- Define inspire and inspiration.

- List two reasons motivation is important.

- List three personal characteristics.

- List two ways a person reveals their character.

- List one risk of characterizing people based on behavior.

- List three values that diverse group members bring to teams.

- List two ways cultural norms vary from one region of the world to another.

Imagine

Since last month, the college sent out hundreds of fliers to the local schools and invited middle and high school students to attend the community fair. The college community relations officer likes your idea so much that she is offering to help. She suggested you put up a demo camp site. She even offered a way to raise money: BBQ shish kabobs and sell them to the public. She's going to give you a prime spot right by the entrance.

One guy's idea to invite a few kids on a campout is taking off. The story got published in the local newspaper and the interview video got noticed by two city council members. One of your group's parents has offered to front the money to buy the food for the fund raiser. A few of your group members are feeling overwhelmed. They haven't done anything like this before.

You know that many of your friends need community service hours during this semester of school. You contact several of them and persuade them that helping with the fundraiser is an easy way to add some hours. Your advisor volunteers to ask other faculty for help.

You know the volleyball team captain is friendly and outgoing. You ask her to take charge of the food. She recruits her entire volleyball team to help prepare the food, and then she persuades a friend who likes to cook to take charge of the BBQ itself.

One of your team members is a little less than excited about the Kamping for Kids idea. He is an Honors student and even received an award last year for not missing a day of school due to illness. You talk him into arranging for the tents and other equipment needed for the demo camp site.

You're still left with group members who think you've all bitten off more than you can chew. You're not sure if they're going to help or not. One of your friends is worried that no one is going to show.

If this event is to succeed, you'll need to consider group members needs and characteristics.

About motivation

As a leader, it's important for you to understand how group members' needs and characteristics affect their participation in the group. Meeting individual's needs and providing an experience that enhances their character is immensely challenging. When you are successful, your team is motivated and anxious to succeed.

Appreciate values

Everyone has values. When the people around you agree with and support your values, you feel like you belong. You're more anxious to see the group succeed. Values are the bottom-line beliefs that drive our character.

List at least six characteristics of values.

Characteristics of values include:

- They are closely held beliefs, usually developed over many years.
- Values don't change readily or quickly.
- They are the standards or principles on which we form attitudes.
- Values aren't the same needs, which is the lack of something desirable.
- Values are usually based on emotions rather than facts.
- Values are the benchmarks that individuals and teams use to choose one behavior over another.
- Values are standards that individuals hold in common and which help sustain the group and its members.
- Team values may or may not be readily identified by team members.

Everyone's values are personal and unique. You probably don't talk about your values much, but they still play a role in all you do.

Focus on common values. To build an effective team, bring individuals together and unite them around a shared set of common values.

List two reasons values are important to a leader.

Values influence everything you do.

Values affect our decisions and behavior. As a leader, don't assume that all members adhere to the same values that you believe. Take time to learn about member's value.

Values influence the information you present. Your organization likely cherishes certain values. As you plan your program, decide if you are presenting these values to your participants. If so, choose specific exercises to help participants identify and learn about those values.

Use learning exercises to draw attention to values. Set the example as a way to communicate your values. Teen youth are usually not mature enough or adequately prepared to facilitate sensitive values clarification exercises. Nonetheless, because of the powerful example set by the youth and adult staff, your program may affect individual's values.

Given the potential impact your program may have on individuals, verify that the learning activities you choose match the values of your sponsor organization.

List two values that high-performing teams usually embrace.

High performing teams develop certain values. Among other values, they value:

- The group as a whole, though not at the expense of an individual.

- Fellow team members, and tell them so in many ways.

- Creativity, autonomy and maturity, and encourage and reward these qualities during the development process and program.

- Life-long learning, believing that individuals are always capable of growing.

Identify norms

Norms are socially acceptable, mutual expectations and rules that guide group members' behavior. They have an immense influence on group performance. Due to the social conditioning behind norms, they are surprisingly motivating.

Sources for norms. Norms are based on:

- The values, expectations, and social needs that members bring with them to the group.

- The history of experiences members gain through participation in your group.

List two types of norms.

Unwritten and informal norms. There are unwritten norms which vary widely between cultural groups.

For example, Americans value direct eye contact. But among Japanese, it is a sign of respect and intense interest to close your eyes while listening to a speaker during a meeting. If you're an American presenting a marketing proposal to a meeting full of Japanese businessmen, you might think that your entire audience has gone to sleep on you!

Unwritten norms include customs or conventions, like being on time for meetings.

In the White Stag program, it's normal to wake at the crack of dawn and run through camp wearing nothing but your swim suit and tennis shoes, shouting "Augi! Augi! Augi!" following someone ringing a loud cowbell, before jumping into a stupendously cold lake.

Mores are related to morality, like wearing a swimsuit at a public beach. Taboos are behavior forbidden by a culture, like first cousins marrying each other.

As a leader, you know that group norms aren't usually written down or even well understood by group members. Still, they exert a powerful influence over group expectations.

Written and formal norms. One set of norms everyone knows about are laws. These are formal rules written and enforced by government. Taboos are usually included in law, although not all mores are. On the Pacific resort island of Mali, a Muslim country, if a woman walks into a restaurant wearing a bikini fresh from the beach, her behavior is strongly offensive, but she won't be arrested.

Identify individual needs

People are motivated by different needs and wants. The most fundamental needs are those that affect our survival.

Define the difference between a need and a want.

The difference between a need and a want is the difference between life and death.

A need is essential. You need elements required for human survival, like food, water, and air.

A want is optional. You want things that make you happier or your circumstances easier, like the latest iPhone.

List four needs common to everyone.

The most basic of people's needs are their survival and psychological needs:

Water. You can go without water for about three days and possibly longer, depending on the environment. Every cell in your body relies on water, and water is essential to maintaining your blood volume. When your blood volume drops too low, your blood pressure collapses and blood stops circulating.

Food. People have survived without food for 3-4 weeks, depending on their physiology and the environmental conditions, though your body begins to break down. Mahatma Gandhi endured several hunger strikes and survived up to 21 days. Irish National Republican Army member Bobby Sands died after 66 days on a hunger strike.

Shelter. In a harsh, cold environment, you may only survive a few hours without shelter. Climbers on Mt. Everest have succumbed to cold within an hour of exposure.

Sleep. In a high school science experiment, 17 year old Randy Gardner didn't sleep for eleven days. But research shows that your memory, judgment, and decision making abilities are impaired after only 24 hours without sleep. Scott Kelley, an Army veteran, wrote that after 36 hours without sleep, his head buzzed, his ability to perform was severely impaired, and he had periods where he could remember nothing. After 48 hours you begin to experience short, involuntary periods of microsleep, like blackouts, and to hallucinate.

Love. Psychologist Renè Spitz studied infants raised in orphanages. He found that if babies were not held, cuddled, and hugged, they did not grow, and if the lack of attention and love continued long enough, even with proper nutrition, they died. The lack of love is emotional abuse. As we grow older, we don't need to be cuddled, but we still need affection, touching, affirmation, and other types of nurturing to feel whole. People who do not feel loved become anti-social and do not thrive.

As a leader, you know your team cannot focus on its goals if they are uncomfortable, hungry, or tired. More importantly, you want to lead them and provide experiences for them that nurture their spirit and being.

Famed psychologist Abraham Maslow conceived of our needs and wants as a pyramid. The bottom of the pyramid contains our survival needs and the top of the pyramid represents our ability to realize our own potential or our capacity to show unselfish concern for other's welfare (*altruism*), as illustrated below. He called this *self-actualization*.

Concern for others

Social needs:
Education, knowledge,
skills and abilities

Psychological and safety needs:
Food, shelter, sleep, warmth, love

Maslow's hierarchy of needs.

List two reasons it's important for a leader to be able to identify his own needs.

Leaders who are self-aware of their own needs are far more effective. There are two reasons it's important to understand what an individual's needs are.

Health and safety. As a leader, it's important to learn about an individual's needs because they affect the person's life. For example:

- An individual with allergies to certain ingredients could die from eating the wrong food.

- You may need to adjust your group's activities to include an individual with a handicap.

- You might need to develop more active learning activities for individuals with short attention spans.

An individual with an attitude problem may need extra encouragement from other group members and extraordinary patience and unqualified love from the staff counselor.

Motives and fears. At a deeper level, if a learner's home life is insecure, their motives and fears about attending your program may be astonishingly different from another person whose home life is relatively stable. The insecure person may attend your program without parental support and is fundamentally seeking affirmation of their self-worth, while the other individual is seeking to exercise skill they already know they possess and greater skill as a leader.

Maslow wrote that fulfilled needs are no longer motivators. When you know what a member's needs are, you understand what motivates them, and you're in a position to exert powerful influence on their success.

List four needs common to virtually everyone.

All group members have common needs. For example, these include:

- Food, warmth, shelter
- Security
- Acceptance
- Belonging
- Recognition

Don't assume based on a few external facts or characteristics that you understand a person's true motives. Exercise your intuition and judgment. You want to build trust and help members of the group reveal their needs and motives. They may not yet even understand their own needs and motives. As a leader, you want to support individuals as they improve their self-awareness.

But be careful when working with people's motives. These are personal traits and people may be easily offended or upset if you're not sensitive to their needs.

Outstanding leaders go out of their way to boost the self-esteem of their personnel. If people believe in themselves, it's amazing what they can accomplish. —Sam Walton

Build self-esteem

You want to not only provide the learner with a tool box of leadership skills, but with a chest of self-esteem. You want to not only help the learner improve his hand and head skills, but grow his heart—empathy, compassion, humility—as well.

You want to improve your ability to learn about and understand team members' needs and motives.

Meet individual's needs

Beyond survival needs, individuals also have certain psychological needs that aren't as easily recognizable, but critical to our physical and emotional well-being nonetheless.

Respect individuals. Individual needs might include, for instance, "doing something challenging or new," "receiving recognition," "fun," "respect from others," and "time alone."

Build loyalty. Given knowledge of a member's needs, the team has a powerful impact as it assists individuals in fulfilling their needs. A team leader who helps individuals meet their needs earns considerable loyalty and commitment from team members. Even under extremely stressful and trying circumstances, if team members feel loyalty to you and their team, they are able perform well beyond their normal comfort zone.

Identify what youth need

List two characteristics of motivation.

Motivation is something that encourages you to behave in a certain way. People are motivated by something they want. It's usually something external like a reward or recognition. For example, to encourage you to achieve goals, your parents might offer you use of the family car.

Short-term rewards. Rewards usually fulfill short-term needs like money, food, shelter, or recognition. For example, a parent might promise their teen who earns high grades $25.00 for every A earned, or they might offer a trip to their favorite pizza joint.

Long-term recognition. Research has proven that money is a relatively short-term motivator, lasting less than six months. What youth most want is greater autonomy and responsibility. This includes taking a trip with another family, staying over at a friends' house, or staying out late. Teens also like sincere praise and recognition, although they may not admit it.

When youth receive a promised reward or recognition, they are more satisfied and happy.

Define inspire and inspiration.

Inspire means to give or receive feelings or thoughts that animate and quicken the spirit.

Inspiration is an internal reward identified by the individual that encourages individuals to assume leadership roles. Intrinsic rewards are specific to an individual and fulfill long-term needs like self-esteem, belonging, personal growth, and a sense of accomplishment.

Inspiration is a natural consequence when a team's vision is aligned with its member's sense of self-esteem and self-worth.

Average leaders give people something to work on. Great leaders give people something to work for. —Simon Sinek

In high-performing teams, leadership is shared among team members and may shift rapidly to accommodate changing environment and circumstances.

- A high-performing team includes individuals who:
- Feel inspired, producing a sustained feeling of increased self-esteem and self-worth.
- Like to work in tight-knit teams and task forces.
- Are inspired by the team's vision and feel loyal to the team.
- Are recognized for their contributions, helping them feel greater satisfaction.

List two reasons motivation is important.

Motivation is important because people:

- Need something bigger that drives them towards goals.
- Can't succeed without understanding what motivates them.

Internal or external. Motives are internally and externally driven. Employees may be motivated by the prospect of a pay increase or a promotion. Entrepreneurs are motivated by the idea of financial independence. A minister may be spurred on by the desire to be of service, to give back because of the support they received along the way.

The power of a person with a vision who is convinced of the righteousness of their idea should not be underestimated. People move mountains when their heart and mind is fully engaged in pursuit of a worthy accomplishment.

Never believe that a few caring people can't change the world. For, indeed, that's all who ever have —Margaret Mead

A worthy vision motivates you to wake up earlier and go to bed later. You're eager to succeed.

Learn personal characteristics

As a leader, you want to learn about the mental and moral qualities that are distinctive to each individual, that make up their character. Learn their temperament, strengths, and weaknesses. These are usually known as your personality.

Recognize personality traits

There are dozens of words that describe personal characteristics or attributes. For example: kind, mature, relaxed, selfless, nervous, and so on.

List three personal characteristics.

Sociologists and psychologists usually classify personality traits into The Big Five.

Openness. This describes how open you are to new ideas, how creative you are, how likely you are to defy convention and custom. If you're always looking for a better way to do something, you're open to new ideas.

Extraversion. This characteristic describes how warm and outgoing you are. If you are spontaneous and love to spend time with lots of friends, you rank high on the extraversion scale.

Agreeableness. This quality takes into account how cooperative, kind, and dependable you are. If you're usually more interested in giving service to others than meeting your needs, you are more agreeable.

Conscientiousness. This attribute refers to how well you're organized, your level of personal discipline, and willingness to take risks. If you are always on time for class and don't forget your homework, you're definitely conscientious.

Neuroticism. Individuals with this trait tend to be more nervous and anxious and less self-confident and content. If you are usually preoccupied about what might happen and tend to worry about issues you don't have control over, you have neurotic traits.

As you might guess, high-performing leaders tend to score higher on the first three attributes, lower on the fourth, and terribly low on the last trait.

List two ways a person reveals their character.

There are several ways people reveal their character.

Based on what they do. For example, if a person is always quite well organized, you might conclude they're disciplined. Watch how they treat others. Notice their personal habits. Compare how they are in private to how they are in public. Contrast their behavior with what they say.

Based on what they say. This is the most direct evidence of people's character. Watch what they say and how they say it. Notice their use and choice of words. But depending on the circumstance, youth pretend to be someone they're not.

Based on what you infer. For example, if a person's clothes look shabby, dirty, or unkempt, you might think that the individual is poor, or, alternatively, that he doesn't care about his appearance. Don't make conclusions based on what you *think* because you might be wildly wrong. Always seek corroborating information.

List one risk of characterizing people based on behavior.

Hidden needs. There is a risk of characterizing people based on their behavior: they have hidden needs that drive their behavior.

For example, someone who wears worn-out clothing may have not learned about the impact their appearance has on how you perceive them. Or their family might be going through a hard time.

It's likely that your group's participants are drawn from a variety of locations and socio-economic backgrounds, and their individual characteristics and perspectives vary.

Knowing individual characteristics, tailor your group's efforts and activities to take advantage of members' talents and interests. You might plan for a volleyball or soccer match after the work is done to satisfy several athletes. More but shorter breaks might be scheduled for the same person who gets restless sitting for long periods.

Seek group diversity

Individuals from diverse socio-economic and cultural backgrounds may have extremely different expectations as group members and leaders. This diversity affects how successful the group is.

A diverse membership may bring considerable value to groups. Members who participate in groups with a diverse cultural mix experience different points of view, ways of thinking, and varying lifestyles.

List three values that diverse group members bring to teams.

Groups with a diverse membership gain several possible advantages:

Improved understanding. Members are less likely to take their own values and beliefs for granted. They improve their understanding of their own limited perceptions and experiences.

More openness. Members become more open to alternative ways of thinking, ideas, and action that otherwise they might not have been considered.

Break conventional wisdom. Members who aren't indoctrinated with existing cultural ways of thinking are more likely to offer unconventional ideas and solutions to problems.

List two ways cultural norms vary from one region of the world to another.

Norms vary widely from one culture to another. Differences in body language may include physical distance, eye contact, suppressing emotions, gestures, touch, posture, silence, physical appearance, and others.

For example:

Decision making. The Japanese culture places value on consensus decision making, in which great effort is expended to engage all members before a decision is reached. On the other hand, many Latin American cultures value hierarchical-based decision making and the authority it demonstrates.

Personal space. In Cairo, Egypt, there's no such thing as personal space. People crowd right up against one another in buses and at breakfast stands. In Tokyo, professional "pushers" cram as many people onto trains as possible. Short people may be wedged in so tightly their feet don't touch the floor. In the United States, it's rude to stand within about 18" of someone.

Hand gestures. In the United States, holding the flat palm upwards with the thumb extended and waving it side to side means to say goodbye. In most European countries, this gesture simply means "no."

Eye contact. In American and European culture, direct eye contact represents directness and honesty. In the Japanese culture, looking someone directly in the eyes is quite aggressive or rude.

Leaders need to be alert to diverse cultural experiences that may influence a member's expectations. By including people from diverse backgrounds who see situations and opportunities differently, you enhance the success of your team. It's worth overcoming the challenges of working with people from different backgrounds and cultures.

English politician and philosopher John Stuart Mill was an early advocate of free markets. In 1848, he wrote *Principles of Political Economy*, in which he stated,

It is hardly possible to overstate the value, in the present low state of human improvement, of placing human beings in contact with persons dissimilar to themselves, and with modes of thought and action unlike those with which they're familiar... Such communication has always been, and is particularly in the present age, one of the primary sources of progress. —John Stuart Mill

Storming the Group

When a group has been in existence long enough to learn about each other, they're beginning to sort out who's in charge and what they are about. The pleasantries of learning about each other give way to a struggle to figure out how to work together.

Once you've helped the group figure out what they stand for and their purpose, the next step is help them work more effectively as a team. Learners have had a chance to practice the first three competencies. Now it's time to move on to the twin tasks of all leaders:

To do the job and keep the group together.

This period in group growth is sometimes a contentious period as differing personalities attempt to dominate key roles in communication and leadership.

Your challenge is to identify learning experiences that not only give them a chance to learn leadership skills, but that also help develop as a team. Your goal is to create a need within group members to know more about leadership and to feel loyalty to their team.

Petty issues conceal real concerns. Sometimes the issues appear petty, but the real struggle is for deeper issues. A few members want to be in control and compete for the role as the designated leader. There is probably tension and disunity present as members clarify what their individual goals are and how their needs are met as a member of the group.

People may bring hidden agendas with them that motivate behavior contrary to group unity. There may be cliques or factions that struggle for dominance.

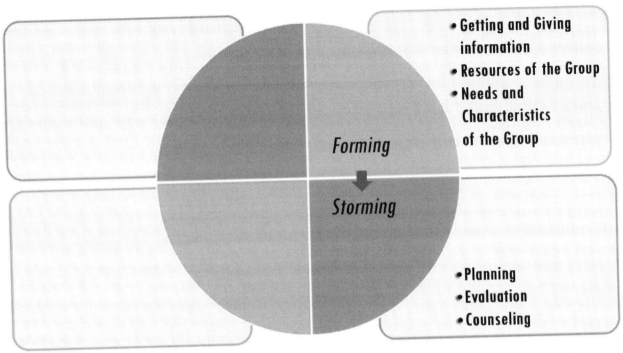

As the group figures out how to work together, they develop their skills in planning, evaluation, and counseling.

Compromises are reached. Group members may fear the group is falling apart even before it's gotten started and a few people may drop out. The group gradually resolves these conflicts as they focus on specific goals. Individuals compromise on personal wants and needs to help advance group goals.

Since keeping the team together is such an important skill, give special attention to the competencies required. These interpersonal skills are complex, require more practice and maturity, more deliberate self-control, and greater willingness to take risks. While essential to storming the group, these competencies are needed throughout the group's life cycle.

Storm the group. To help the group sort out their differences and become more unified, plan learning activities using these leadership skills:

- **Planning.** As an effective leader, you are often called on to problem-solve, to make decisions, and to consider and implement complex plans.

- **Evaluation.** As a leader, you must know where your team is headed and continually assess what's working, what needs to change, and what's not working.

- **Counseling.** Listening, coaching, and offering personal feedback is a complex and subtle skills, requiring probably a high degree of personal integration, practice, and experience. It's entirely people oriented, except to the degree an individual might need counseling to resolve a task-oriented problem.

Planning

About planning

Planning is a process of anticipating and organizing activities to achieve a desired goal. Planning is usually proactive, in advance of starting an activity.

Your decision at each step helps clarify your choices in the next step. Planning is useful in group situations, one-on-one, and individually.

Planning is developing a sequence of action steps that have to occur for you to achieve your goal. When you plan effectively, you reduce the time and effort required to achieve your goal. A plan is like a map. It allows you to track your progress towards the goal.

When you engage in a structured planning process, you're more confident about the information you gather and the decision you make based on that information. Your clarity of judgment is improved and you're able to make firm decisions.

Planning is an essential activity in all types of professions and trades. As you grow older and assume more responsibility in life and leadership roles in your family, community and work life, planning becomes increasingly important to your success.

Planning is an iterative, cyclical process. This means as you move forward you may gain new information that alters what you do next. This new information may require you to adjust your existing plan. Capable leaders are skilled at adapting to evolving circumstances.

Planning is a core competency. It offers a general conceptual framework to integrate a variety of related skills, including:

- Problem-solving
- Scheduling
- Time management
- Project management
- Performance appraisal
- Negotiation
- Conflict resolution

Planning is such an important skill that universities and colleges offer all types of planning degrees in fields like financial planning, urban planning, logistics, and management.

Objectives

When you complete presenting the content in this chapter, learners are able to:

- Name five occupations that use planning.
- List three elements that are common to planning and problem-solving.
- List three goals of planning.
- List three principles that help you develop an effective plan.
- Define three characteristics of a vision.
- Define three characteristics of a goal.
- List the seven steps of planning.
- Draw a diagram of the basic planning process.
- List four reasons why it's important to take time to plan.
- List four techniques for clarifying the task.
- List four basic types of resources.
- List three ways to identify and prioritize your resources.
- List two reasons it's necessary to consider alternatives when planning.
- Name two ways that planning contributes to group success.

- List two steps that help your team to make good decisions.

- List four reasons to write down your plan.

- Describe two methods to communicate your plan.

- List two techniques to help you keep your plan on track.

Imagine

Your group has progressed since you were interviewed by the local newspaper a month ago. The fundraiser drew attention and five more people from another high school came to your last meeting. Three of them are still active. Two more adults volunteered to help.

The mother of one of your members is a director of a local volunteer service organization. She's offered to help you apply for a grant from her organization that could mean a big boost to your group's goal of putting on a week-long Kamping for Kids program next summer.

To qualify for the grant, you have to show the service organization that you've thought issues and challenges through. Develop an outline a plan for your summer camp as if it's going to take place and find a possible location.

List and prioritize supplies and gear. That includes food for 40 people for a week: 12 group members, 2 adults, and 26 participants. List people and the roles they will fill during the summer event. You have to decide who's going to be in charge. You have to advertise and market your program. You have a small budget, so you have to keep your plans reasonably sized to start.

The deadline for the grant application is only one month away. How are you going to gather the information necessary, consider your options, and make all these decisions by then?

You need good planning skills if you're going to meet that deadline and obtain funding.

Why plan

Planning is something you do all the time. Use these steps to prepare an effective plan.

List three elements that are common to planning and problem-solving.

Planning, problem-solving, and decision-making have a lot in common. Among other characteristics, they all require you to:

- Assess the situation.
- Consider alternatives.
- Make decisions.

List three goals of planning.

Planning helps you to improve:

- The quality of the decisions made.
- Team members' skills and abilities.
- The results achieved.

By following a proven planning structure, you improve the number and quality of options available to you at each step of the process. This produces improved outcomes.

Planning is bringing the future into the present so that you can do something about it now. —Alan Lakein

Name five occupations that use planning.

Virtually every occupation uses planning, every day. Planning applies to everything you do.

List three principles that help you develop an effective plan.

When making decisions, applying a few key principles enhances the problem-solving process.

Present a win/win attitude. Remind group members that everyone wins when the group is successful.

Strive to obtain input and agreement from everyone. Avoid formal "majority" voting, which creates a win/lose experience.

Apply each planning step deliberately. Seek members' agreement before moving to the next step. Don't skip a step.

Break the task into smaller pieces. Solve little problems and create little successes first, before tackling the "big" problem.

Don't fixate on a single problem or one possible solution. If the group gets stuck on an issue or possible solution, clarify the areas of agreement and non-agreement.

Summarize areas of agreement. Focus on progress achieved. If the group is stuck, back up to the point and level of generality where the group previously reached agreement.

Develop your vision and goals

Before you can plan, you need to know where you're headed and what you want to accomplish. You need a vision—and meaningful goals and objectives.

A man who does not think and plan long ahead will find trouble right at his door. — *Confucius*

Identify your vision

It takes time for a group to grow until it's ready to identify its vision. That doesn't mean you must wait for a vision before you begin progress. But you must be able to describe what you want to accomplish. So you might start with a high-level goal that summarizes your greater purpose.

Define three characteristics of a vision.

An effective vision statement:

Is short, simple, and compelling. A vision statement is a short, simple, compelling, idealized description of a worthy long-term accomplishment. Your vision is a condensed statement of the passion that drives your organization. The fewer the words, the better.

For example, 10,000 Youth Learning Leadership Yearly.

Embodies what you believe. A vision statement embodies your organization's core values, scope, and intent. It's a foundation around which the organization organizes its work. It provides a "why" for all that work.

Is future-oriented. A vision statement communicates an ideal state that is up to several years ahead. It provides long-term direction for your organization.

Every great dream begins with a dreamer. Always remember, you have within you the strength, the patience, and the passion to reach for the stars to change the world. –*Harriet Tubman*

Is unifying. A vision statement is a unifying declaration of intent. It articulates something significant that your organization wants to achieve. It's an expression of a future, idealized state. It's an aspirational, inspiring statement. It's a summary picture of what your organization would be doing when it attains its purpose. A vision represents a long-term commitment by the organization.

A vision statement is personal to the organization. It usually takes time, up to several months or even years, for teams to gain enough maturity, unity, and purpose before they're ready to define their vision.

Requires time to conceive. Developing a vision statement that accurately reflects the intent of your team is challenging. Articulating your vision isn't easy. It requires soul-searching by team members and give and take. Ideally, every team member embraces the organization's vision.

A vision isn't something your team can describe during their first meeting, or a new leader presents to the team shortly after joining an organization.

A vision is fed by your waking dreams. Dreams are a source of creative imagination you can use to fuel your desires and ambitions. Refuse to be average. Don't give up on your dreams. They are the place to start identifying your vision.

You don't have to see the whole staircase, just take the first step. —Martin Luther King, Jr.

A vision isn't constrained by available resources or limitations. That's what goals are for.

Define goals

A goal is an achievement that moves you closer to your vision. It's a general statement describing your desired expectations or results. It's a benchmark that describes an achievable future state.

Many dictionaries and other sources use the words *goal* and *objective* interchangeably. Definitions of objective include "A goal or purpose;" "A thing aimed at or sought; a goal;" and, "Something that one's efforts or actions are intended to attain or accomplish; purpose; goal; target." Many people confuse the two.

An architect has a vision of the completed house. Completing the foundation, framing, sheetrock, exterior, roofing, and painting are a series of goals. Figuring out how many boxes of nails you'll need is an objective.

Define three characteristics of a goal.

Characteristics of effective goals:

Describe your direction and purpose. Effective goals are a link between your group's future vision—which isn't possible today—and what you want to accomplish. Goals pull the team forward, defining where you want to go.

Transform your vision into action. Goals move your organization forward. They help you solve problems and stretch the organization's capacity.

Constrained by available resources. Unlike a vision, goals are anchored in your current situation and based on reality. That doesn't mean that your goals are limited by available resources or constraints. They identify and help resolve challenges that help your group to grow and prosper.

Narrow your vision. When you define a goal, you're refining your vision. While a vision is unconstrained by reality, goals respond to reality and strive to change it. Revise and update your goals to reflect shifting external circumstances, completed steps, and changes in scope.

Are time-bound. Goals describe outcomes or results achievable in multiple weeks or months, typically less than two years. Your goals identify who and what: the audience and the result.

Objectives are very specific. For details on writing objectives, see Present the objectives on page 207.

If you don't have time to write down your goals, where are you going to find the time to accomplish them? —Sid Savara

Seven steps of planning

List the seven steps of planning.

- Planning has seven steps or phases.

- Consider the task

- Consider the resources

- Generate alternatives

- Reach a decision

- Write your plan down

- Implement your decision
- Evaluate

Draw a diagram of the basic planning process.

The planning process is a simple six step wheel.

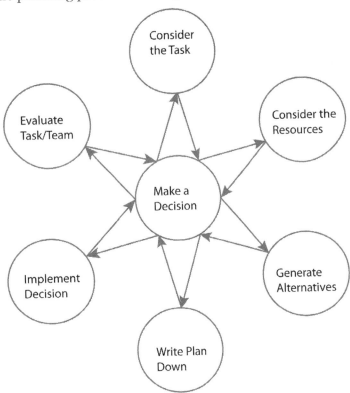

The planning process.

Consider the task

List four reasons why it's important to take time to plan.

To do what's right. When you make decisions in a hurry, you may regret your actions. Think through your decisions and their possible short- and long-term consequences. This allows you to make ethical, responsible, thoughtful decisions. Stop what you're doing and take time to plan. Team members are confident that their actions support the team's vision, goals, principles, values, and ethics.

Give me six hours to chop down a tree and I will spend the first four sharpening the axe. – Abraham Lincoln

Support team values and ethics. Developing a plan reminds team members that their values and ethics are important. A plan converts the team member's values and members' ideas into solutions that produce desired results.

List resources and limitations. A plan helps team members identify available resources, both internal and external, affecting the issue.

Get agreement on the problem. A plan helps team members to confirm that they're working on the same problem before beginning to identify solutions. Team members commit to the task and a solution with a clear understanding of their responsibility and role.

Avoid crisis-reaction mode. Effective planning allows the group to act before problems are too large or reach crisis mode. Group members act proactively, anticipating potential problems, rather than react after the fact in fire-fighting mode.

Get team members commitment. Allow team members to talk about their understanding of the task, problems, misunderstandings, and feelings. This lessens the chance to misunderstandings and resentment later on.

Focus on the solution. Helps team members focus on the solution rather than the problem and on the task and not individuals. This helps bring the group together and focus on the task.

Designate a leader. A plan clearly establishes ownership of and responsibility for the problem.

Planning is both work and progress. Sometimes people don't think they're making progress unless they're "doing something." Planning isn't always recognized as valuable work because the results aren't tangible. Taking the time to formally plan acknowledges that the preparation is as important as the execution.

List four techniques for clarifying the task.

As you consider the task, use these techniques to clarify the group's task and clarify what is most important. Words in "quotes" are suggested phrases for a facilitator or leader.

Techniques	Description
Identify Who, What, When, and Why	Get specific.
Legitimize Team Member's Feelings	Accept that individual perceptions may vary, even if you don't agree with them.
	Accept that may view the issue as a problem while others may not.

Techniques	Description
How Does it Feel?	Get to the emotional parts of the issue: "Can you tell the group how you feel about facing this issue every day?"
	What's the real problem?
	If you can't resolve group or member resistance:
	Ask clarifying questions: "Is there anything about the problem that you disagree with?
	Speak the unspeakable: "I don't feel like you're describing the real problem. What is the real issue?"
	Float a trial balloon: "I'm not at all sure this is right—isn't the real problem that you have a dislike for the way Joe dresses?"
Best/Worst/Most Probable	Back into the issue:
	"What is the absolute worst thing that could happen because of solving the problem?"
	"What is the best outcome you can think of?" "What is the most likely outcome?"
	"Can we try for 10 minutes to tackle this problem? We might still come up with something new."
	"What is the worst possible outcome if we take no action?"
Ownership	Who owns the problem? What is your relationship to the owner? Are they in a position of authority to you?
	Get the right people committed: "Should this group tackle this problem at all? Today or later on? Who else should be involved? Who has responsibility? Is this a challenge our group can handle?
State Problem as a Question	Instead of, "Plan a hike to the top of the mountain", you can ask, "Why do we need to hike to the top of the mountain?"
	Ask open-ended (not Yes/No) questions. "Could you put that in terms of 'How to...'?" For example, do you mean, "How can the group be more sensitive to...?"
Problem as Given/Problem as Understood	Clarify the problem: "How do *I* define it vs. how does *he* define it?" "That's the problem as described by the hurdle card. Is there anything missing?" Are group members making any assumptions about the problem?

Techniques	Description
Lasso	Narrow the focus and get down to specifics: "Could you clarify what you mean by, 'The ultimate camping experience?' "
Is/Is not	Eliminate assumptions: "Which of our goals is definitely not affected by the situation?"
Diagram	People are better visual thinkers. Try moving from verbal to visual: "Maria, why don't you draw a sketch of the bridge you think we should build?" Draw out interactions, dependencies, and relationships affected by the problem and possible solutions.
Focus on connections, relationships	Look at related tasks and people and assess potential impacts on them. "So if we apply the new organizational structure we've outlined, does it affect all the groups we've diagrammed here? Did we leave any groups out?"

Consider the resources

List four basic types of resources.

The purpose of the second step of planning, *consider the resources*, is to determine the human, physical, monetary, and time resources available to the group.

People's knowledge, skills, and abilities: "Do we have all the skills needed within our group? Who can do this lashing? Who's managed building a bridge before? Are there any skills we're going to need help on from outside the group?"

Physical resources in the environment: "Let's be creative for a moment. Are there resources around you that you can use instead of rope to fasten the poles together? What about using ivy?"

Money: "How much money is there in the budget for the task?"

Time: "We have two hours to hike five miles to the top of Pico Blanco. Can we do it?"

List three ways to identify and prioritize your resources.

As you consider your resources, use the following techniques to clarify what is most important. Words in "quotes" are suggested phrases for a facilitator or leader.

Techniques	Description
Ask basic questions	*Who, what, why, when, where, how*: "When do we have to complete the task? Have we been given a location to cut the trees for the tower?"
Urgent/ Important	Is the task urgent, important or both? Is there a deadline? Who set the deadline? Is the deadline absolute, or is it flexible? What are the consequences if we miss the deadline?
Assess limits	"Are there any limitations imposed by the physical environment?" "Does the physical location offer new types of solutions?" "What, if anything, limits possible solutions?" "How much time is available?" "Who can we reach out to for assistance?"
Focus on parts of the problem	"Is there a limiting factor here? Can we do this in only eight hours?"
Break it down	Work to reduce an issue to a manageable size. Break it down into bite-size chunks. "This is a complex issue. Let's take it a piece at a time."
Reducing problems into parts	"It appears we've identified two distinct issues. Can we tackle one at a time? This makes it more manageable."
Force Field Analysis	Ask the group to list in one column the forces for making the decision and in a second column the forces against making the decision. Assign a score to each item: 1 for a weak reason, 5 for a strong reason.
Generalize/ Exemplify	Move from the general to the specific, and from the specific to general: "Could you give us an example of poor communication?" "You've mentioned some examples. How would you describe the general problem?"
Ask the Expert	Avoid rumors and reinventing the wheel: "Is there anyone here who can answer that question?" "Has anyone done this before?"
Best Use	Given the available resources, is this the best use of these resources?

Consider the alternatives

The purpose of the third step of planning, consider the alternatives, is to develop a variety of options (job-related) and keep the group focused (group-related).

List two reasons it's necessary to consider alternatives when planning.

Among the reasons it's necessary to consider alternatives are:

List a wide variety of possible solutions. Developing alternatives helps you have a ready "Plan B" in the wings helps you prepare for when plans go wrong.

Get everyone's input. Taking time to seek everyone's input allows you to tap into the diverse body of resources offered by your team members.

Take time needed. Team members need to consider the problem and possible solutions.

Make an uninformed decision. Alternatives help avoid premature movement towards a solution.

Name two ways that planning contributes to group success.

Help build commitment. When people contribute and participate in decisions. They're more committed to the results and less disturbed when the results aren't as expected.

Carefully evaluate ideas. Thinking through your alternatives allows you to carefully consider your options, possible outcomes, and be sure they meet your team's goals, values, and ethics.

As you consider alternatives ideas, use the following techniques to clarify which are best. Words in "quotes" are suggested phrases for a facilitator or leader.

Techniques	Description
Think "outside the box"	Don't limit yourself to preconceived solutions. Welcome innovative or creative solutions. Don't rely on tradition as the only source for ideas. Don't judge new ideas, welcome them, and reward members for offering them.
Brainstorming	Use brainstorming to generate a large quantity of ideas. Don't think about the quality and don't judge ideas. Piggyback or flip-flop on each other's ideas to generate more ideas. Once you've generated a good quantity of ideas, then condense, consolidate, and categorize ideas. Prioritize and rank options.
Checkerboard	Cross-checking alternatives: "Let's compare each alternative against

	each other. Perhaps we'll see new ideas we hadn't thought of."
Cross-checking against criteria	"We earlier defined a number of points any solution we propose must meet. What do you say we look at that list and see if that stimulates any new ideas?"
Cross-checking task elements	"There are three different peaks we could hike to, and we could take two or three days. Why don't we see what routes there are for all these combinations?"
Cut Up and Move Around	For dealing with physical relationships or sequences: "Why doesn't each of us individually list on cards all the activities between now and the end of the project? Then we'll rank order them as a group."
Experience	Build on past; adapt, modify, etc. "'Who knows what hurdles have been used in this situation in the past?"
Rank Order	Pick the best of the bunch: "Out of the seven solutions proposed, let's each choose three."
Sort by Category	Breaking down the alternatives: "There are about 25 ideas here. Can someone suggest categories they might fit into?"
Evaluating categories	"Are there a few people who would like to sift these ideas into categories and prepare an evaluation of the categories?"
Straw vote	Take a poll or test vote to test group member's commitment to a possible solution or idea. Try negative voting: ask group members to list the possible solutions or ideas that appeal to them least and eliminate them from your choices.
Advantage/ Disadvantage	Draw three columns; label them Pros, Cons, and Outcomes: "We've come down to two basic plans. Why don't we first list the pluses and minuses of Plan A, and then do the same for Plan B?" Then list possible consequences in the third column. Sometimes the volume of one column over the other is suggestive of a possible choice.
"What I like about..."	Give positive feedback first: "If we say what we like first about each of the ideas, it helps us see the positive aspects of each idea and make it easier to find a solution."

Make a decision

List two steps that help your team to make good decisions.

The purpose of the fifth step of planning, *make a decision*, is to:

Confirm agreements made. The team has already made a number of decisions. Reconfirm with them that they agree with the decisions made up to this point.

Confirm members' participation. When you take a moment to confirm their agreement, you help confirm their participation in the solution.

Celebrate progress. Making a decision is the transition point between preparation and action. Planning is hard and valuable work. Take a moment to congratulate the team on their progress.

As you consider alternatives ideas, use the following techniques to clarify which are best. Words in "quotes" are suggested phrases for a facilitator or leader.

Techniques	Description
Get consensus	Verify that all group members agree on the decision reached.
Validate the decision	Verify with group members that they agree with the solution they identified.
Review values	Re-confirm that the decision reached conforms to the group's values, goals, standards, policies, and ethics.

Write plan down

List four reasons to write down your plan.

The purpose of the sixth step of planning, *write the plan down*, is to:

Identify who is in charge. Attach names to specific parts of the project.

List resources. Be specific about the resources you use, including where they're, who has access to them, etc.

Confirm agreement. A written plan is easy to understand and formalizes agreement by team members.

Develop a schedule. A written schedule helps everyone to stay on track.

Improve team success. A written plan helps keep the group together and get the job done.

By failing to prepare, you are preparing to fail. — Benjamin Franklin

Describe two methods to communicate your plan.

As you consider alternatives ideas, use the following techniques to communicate your plan. Words in "quotes" are suggested phrases for a facilitator or leader.

Techniques	Description
Publish the Plan	Write the plan down in a format everyone can both access and understand. This helps avoid misunderstandings and missteps.
List Resources	Write down the resources you're using, whether they're resources, time, money, people, or places. Make sure the group agrees the list is correct.
Post a Schedule	Write down a schedule of who's going to do what and when it's scheduled. If your plan is complex, write down any interdependencies or prerequisites.

Put decision into effect

List two techniques to help you keep your plan on track.

There are several techniques available to help you stay on track.

Track your progress. Describe each step clearly and write it down. Put due dates by each step. Add the name of the person responsible for each step. Check in frequently to identify roadblocks early. Implement alternative plans when unexpected events occur. If possible, chart your progress. Use a piece of paper on the wall, or an app, whatever works for you. Monitor group morale and praise success.

Delegate tasks. Share the load and share leadership where possible. Divide up and multiply your efforts.

Take notes. As you progress, take complete and accurate notes to help you follow up.

As you put your decision into effect, use the following techniques to help stay on course. Words in "quotes" are suggested phrases for a facilitator or leader.

Techniques	Description
Concurrent Evaluation	Check in with group: "Keeping in mind our original criteria or objectives for the choice, how are we doing?"
Stop, Start, Continue	As you implement your plan, look for what's working and what's not working.
Monitor Performance	"Are all group members actively involved? What is the deviation from the plan? Is it positive/negative?"
Share Leadership	"Who is in charge? Is it a shared—or is one person in charge? "What style of leadership is the designated leader using? Is it appropriate to the situation?"
Keeping Team Together/ Getting the Job Done	Strike a balance: Is someone/Are team members continually sensitive to what's happening within the team? Who's checking to make sure there's a positive balance between group and task priorities?

Evaluation

Evaluation, the fifth step of planning, is an assessment of what worked, what didn't work and what you want to change. Find out what you've learned within your group.

After you complete implementing your plan, use the following techniques to evaluate your success. Words in "quotes" are suggested phrases for a facilitator or leader.

Techniques	Description
Feedback	Try for both a group discussion, a record of the results, and a chance for individual members to contribute written comments.
Strengths/ Weaknesses	What to look for: "What does the group feel are the strengths of the project as implemented?" "The weaknesses...?"
Improvements/ Feed-forward	Making it better: "Is there anything we might have done better? How can we improve it next time?" Pass it on: "How can we make sure that future groups benefit from our

experience?"

This is an extremely brief summary of Evaluation. For complete details, see the next chapter, *Evaluation*.

Evaluation

About Evaluation

Evaluation is one of the most important leadership competencies a leader needs and an essential part of ongoing learning. Evaluation begins by defining where you want to go.

Your growth as a leader depends on your willingness to continually improve and change. But before you evaluate, you have to know where you're going. Evaluation allows you to determine if you're progressing. If you want to know if you're moving forward, you have to write down your goals and objectives.

Evaluation is an ongoing skill that is linked to everything you do. When planning, you have to continually evaluate your alternatives. When controlling the group, you have to continually evaluate team member's contributions. As a team progresses towards their selected solution, continually apply what you learn in real time. When the project is complete, be sure to apply what you learned to the next relevant situation.

Objectives

When you complete presenting the content in this chapter, learners are able to:

- List three specific criteria to consider when evaluating.

- List two factors of group success that you want to continually evaluate.

- List three different types of learning you want to evaluate.

- List five issues you must consider when you evaluate the group.

- List a positive method to recognize team member's contributions.

- Describe the best time to formally evaluate any situation.

- List one advantage of sharing what you learned from your evaluation.

- List three reasons to publicly share progress towards objectives.

- List at least three different methods used to evaluate alternatives.

Imagine

Your group put considerable effort into the presentation to the local service organization a month ago. You are hoping they will give you a grant that will help your Kamping for Kids idea started.

Most of your efforts were successful. You came up with a list of supplies and resources but when you made the presentation you realized you forgot some important items like first aid supplies. You didn't think about finding someone with medical skill. You came up with an outline for what you wanted to complete during Kamping for Kids. The service group complimented you on your budget plan. But when members of the service organization asked specific questions, you didn't have all the answers.

Your group was embarrassed when you left the meeting with the service group. You were told you would hear from them in a two or three weeks. Four weeks have gone by and you still haven't heard anything. Group members are, without saying it, blaming each other. They are focused on what didn't work.

What are your options now? How do you move forward? How can you figure out where you made mistakes and how to fix them? Was it someone's fault? How do you identify what the group did right? How will you correct the faults and come up with a revised plan that fills in the holes? Is there still a chance you'll receive the grant?

Evaluate what happened, identify what worked and didn't work, and make changes.

Maintain an evaluation attitude

Progress towards objectives. Continually assess how the group is progressing towards its objectives. Imagine an eagle soaring on the wind: it's constantly testing, consciously and unconsciously, wind current, flow, altitude, strength, time, direction, and position relative to where it wants to go.

Continuous improvement. You're committed to continually examine and analyze your progress towards completing your objectives. An evaluation attitude sharpens your team's awareness of their progress and helps you motivate and guide them. If the autopilot on your aircraft doesn't continually correct itself, you won't reach your destination.

List two factors of group success that you want to continually evaluate.

Consider both how well you're keeping the team together and completing the task. An effective team cares about both getting the job done and helping everyone succeed. If you only do one or the other, you're not building an effective, sustainable team.

Continually evaluate two factors of group success:

Getting the job done. Ok, sometimes people go through the paces. If that's all you expect, that's probably what you're getting. The job gets done well enough, but does that mean the group was successful?

Keeping the team together. Develop a feeling for the health of the team members and the team. No, not whether anyone has a cold. You want to know how they feel about their membership on your team. You want to know if they're chillin', taking up space, or are they actually committed to the team's goals. If you watch how people interact, you learn a lot about whether they feel like they belong.

What to evaluate

List three specific criteria to consider when evaluating.

Every evaluation needs to consider three specific criteria:

- **Start.** What should we start doing? Focus on the learners. To stimulate discussion, ask open-ended questions such as, "If time and limited resources aren't a factor, what else should we be doing?" List new ideas that participants believe need to be included next time. Discuss topics you want to cover next time. When considering adding new content, assess whether it's specific to the existing participants or generic to all learners. Identify activities that failed to contribute to completing objectives.

- ***Stop!*** List what isn't working, what's broken, failures, and frustrations. Assess whether you should stop presenting a specific topic of a method of presentation. Look for activities that consume time but don't provide equal or greater return. Identify activities and events that might be fun but aren't purposeful and distract from more useful learning activities. List experiences that have been overused that you want to put on the back shelf for a while.

- **Continue.** Identify what's working well. Encourage ideas by asking, "What are we doing that's making a difference?" "What had the most impact on participants?" Look for activities that stand out. Consider events that emotionally affected learners. List the experiences that contributed most to your objectives. Identify activities that are marginally successful and list ways to modify and improve them for next time.

Consider your objectives

When you evaluate, consider your objectives.

Measure your progress. One of your most important challenges is to help your team members grow. That means you're willing to grow, which translates into evaluation. Learning to analyze, evaluate, and plan for improvement is incredibly important.

As a leader, you're always striving to find a balance between getting the job done and keeping the team together. In practice, the group members' needs and their effectiveness at getting the job done varies over time. Moving from the start to the finish isn't a straight line. Like taking a hike, you have to wander over a few hills and climb out of a few valleys to get where you're going.

Evaluate learning

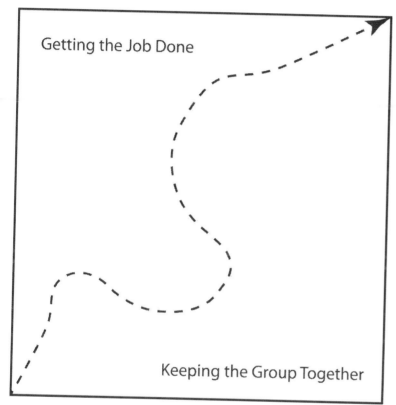

Leadership an ongoing challenge: getting the job done and keeping the team together.

List three different types of learning you want to evaluate.

When you write down your goals and objectives, consider how you are developing your team members' hands, head, and heart skills. It's challenging to think about, write down, and measure team members' success in completing your goals and objectives in all three areas.

Hands. You can observe hands-on skills, which makes them relatively easy to quantify. You can watch and assess whether a learner has accomplished the objective.

Example. "The learner must build a fire that they light using only one match and boil a quart of water within five minutes."

Head. It's more difficult to evaluate whether a learner has gained new knowledge. You need indirect evidence that demonstrates the learner has acquired and is able to apply the information.

Example. "List the five steps of problem-solving. Then, using the resources provided, develop a written plan to build a foot bridge across the creek 300 yards below the supply hut. You have 45 minutes to complete the plan."

Heart. It's very difficult to quantify a person's attitude. Attitudes are nebulous and impossible to directly observe. The best method, if you have the means and time, is to survey learners before and after they participate in your program. But conducting social studies is often unrealistic for small organizations.

As a leader of a youth program, one of your goals may be to develop goals and objectives that enable participants to embrace the spirit and meaning of your program. An alternative to expensive social surveys is to provide experiences designed to influence individual attitudes.

Example. "Each learner will participate in a welcoming ceremony during which they are asked to write down their greatest fear during the program. Instruct the learner to seal the statement in an envelope. At the end of the program, conduct a reflection ceremony during which learners are given the opportunity to open their envelope and talk about that fear."

Without expensive surveys and social studies to assess how participants' attitudes change, you're only able to rely on anecdotal feedback. Support this by asking learners for written reviews and comments.

Evaluate the task

List five issues to consider when you evaluate the task.

There are at least five issues to consider when you evaluate the task:

- Did the results meet our expectations and objectives? How does it differ? If it differs is it better or worse than the original plan? What is the quality of the product? How does it look?

- Was it done on time?

- Did you choose the best alternative?

- What did you like least/most about the job?

- How could you improve next time (in the same or a similar situation)?

- Did you accurately anticipate potential problems?
- Did you use our resources to the fullest extent possible?
- Is there another way to do this you hadn't thought of?

When you evaluate, it's easy to think a lot about the job and harder to evaluate the people. Evaluate both.

Evaluate the group

List five issues you must consider when you evaluate the group.

There are five issues you must consider when you evaluate the group.

When evaluating the group, consider:

- **Was everyone involved**? Did all of the team members make reasonable contribution? Why or why not? How do group members feel about their contribution?
- **Are team members satisfied with the result**? Why or why not? What was the spirit of the group?
- **Did the group work well together?** Would you like to work together again? Why or why not?
- **Communication**. Was it effective and clear?
- **Identify the leader**. Who was in charge? Why?
- **Identify weaknesses.** How can you strengthen the group's and member's weaknesses?

Evaluate individuals

Highly effective teams place value on the worth and integrity of every individual. Leaders must be aware of peoples' differences. They must be aware that all individuals need success experiences.

People are more successful when they can compare their own progress against personal standards and not those of a universal "average" or "best." If the individual knows how he stands relative to standards he helped develop, then he is more motivated to keep on trying.

Focus on what worked

List a positive method to recognize team member's contributions.

Focus on the positive. Positive recognition is much more effective than focusing on what didn't work. Research has shown that both children and adults are more successful when their positive contributions are recognized then when their failures are highlighted. Work hard to be sure participants know what you want and recognize them when they achieve it.

Evaluate whenever it's needed

Describe the best time to formally evaluate any situation.

During and after the event. Hold formal evaluation sessions as needed. For example, you ought to evaluate daily, usually at the end of each day of your leadership program. Your staff needs to meet every night to evaluate that day's program, review and make adjustments to the following day's schedule, and so forth.

The purpose of evaluation is to gather information. Think about the information you want to gather and what you want to do with it. Otherwise you may end up with so much information you may not be able to analyze it effectively or gather too little to be useful.

Share what you learned

Sometimes people are tempted to keep the results of an evaluation private. They fear negative consequences, or that individuals may be hurt by the conclusions, or that the team might look bad.

List one advantage of sharing what you learned from your evaluation.

Avoid keeping secrets. In truth, there are no secrets. Everyone associated with the team already knows what happened – for good and bad. Keeping your conclusions secret undermines continued confidence in your team, because it appears that no one is learning any lessons.

Post results publicly

One extremely effective evaluation technique is to share the results publicly. During the workshop, mount a wall chart or poster that lists your objectives. This can be in form of a check off list, a grid, a chart, or other visual aid.

List three reasons to publicly share progress towards objectives.

There are good reasons to post every team's progress in completing objectives:

Increase participant's knowledge. Posting evaluation results publicly helps everyone improve their knowledge of goals and objectives.

Lists accomplishments by group. Posting objectives adds an element of competition, as every team can see their progress—or lack of—relative to all the other groups. It encourages groups to achieve greater results.

Communicate objectives publicly. Written objectives that everyone can see communicate what's expected. Use simple, factual, measurable language that participants understand.

Give responsibility to every member. When you are asked to evaluate what you know or don't know, you are immediately interested in knowing what you're expected to be able to measure. Members are engaged in and more responsible for their own learning.

Make the objectives central to success. Asking team members to evaluate their success brings the objectives to the forefront of the program. It raises their awareness of the objectives and their central role in whether the learners got something out of the program.

Because of the competitive spirit, caution learners against checking objectives that aren't yet complete. The groups should conduct the evaluation in the presence and with the input of the youth staff. Their presence helps preserve the integrity and honesty of the evaluation process.

Example: You wrote several objectives that require the team to learn about and use each other's resources. You developed an activity based on those objectives. Give each team a list of the objectives for the learning activity. List the objectives and the activity in a grid for each team. Ask the learners to rate as a team their overall success in completing each objective and the activity. Ask the team to place a check in each grid they completed.

Visible results. With you post results in a central, public place, everyone quickly sees their progress and how their team compares to the others. The entire staff sees at a glance the success of their overall plan. Now you know *exactly* which objectives each group has completed.

Get instant feedback. Everyone can instantly visualize their team's progress towards accomplishing the objectives. You don't need to wait until your staff meeting or until the program ends to find out if you completed your objectives. Using this real-time feedback, consider whether to modify your program immediately.

Evaluation methods

List at least three different methods used to evaluate alternatives.

Several potential evaluation methods are described below.

Evaluation Method	Description
Criteria Checkerboard	A criteria checkerboard is a simple method for comparing criteria against each other.

	A	B	C	D	E	F	G	...
1								
2								
3								
...								

	Criteria are explicitly listed. Compare against alternatives, one-for-one, until all criteria and alternatives have been compared.
	This may result in a yes/no comparison, a ranking of relative merit, or in prioritizing certain factors.
	List all alternatives on both axis, allowing you to compare like criteria to like criteria. One alternative may become more preferable to others.
Rank order	Out of all the alternatives, the group votes for a specified number to determine which are preferred.
Sort by category	This is a way to group alternatives to allow you to sort them more easily. Once the choices are categorized, you may be able to eliminate the entire group without having to consider each member of the group.
Advantages/ disadvantages	List the pluses and minuses for each option. Are there any advantages or disadvantages that automatically eliminate an option?
"What I like about..."	Stating a positive opinion first builds support for solving the problem. It also forces members to look at the positive aspects which are contained in most ideas.

Counseling

About counseling

Counseling is a compassionate, private talk between individuals that helps someone resolve personal problems.

As a leader, you're sensitive to people's need. They may come to you with a problem, or you may sense they have an issue. You can't turn them away or let the problem grow, because you care about your team members. You also know that when individual problems are ignored, they become the group's problem. A problem that was initially limited to one person is now limiting the entire team.

Counseling is a difficult skill to learn. Professional counselors, like lawyers, investment bankers, clergymen, vocational counselors, and psychiatrists spend years to learn how to counsel in their fields. People often pay large amounts of money to receive expert counsel.

As youth leaders, depending on the complexity of the issue, your job isn't to solve their problem. You rarely have more than 15 or 20 minutes to talk. Your job is to offer first aid, to help them resolve small problems on the spot. If they need ongoing help, or if you feel the issues are bigger, encourage the individual to seek help from their parents or a trusted adult.

Objectives

When you complete presenting the content in this chapter, learners are able to:

- List three occasions when counseling is appropriate.

- List three behaviors that show counseling is needed.

- Define two parts of first aid counseling.

- Identify the most important skill of counseling.

- State the most important safeguard you must take as a counselor.

- List at least two ways to let people know that they have your undivided attention.

- List five non-verbal channels of communication.

- List three characteristics of reflective listening.

- List two behaviors that legitimize another person's feelings.

- List three reasons it's not a good idea to offer advice.

- List three ways to offer encouragement and add information.

Imagine

During your camping trip last month, one of your members fell and sprained his ankle. Your group debated back and forth whether to keep going the last half-mile to the camp site or quit and go home.

No one could agree on what to do. The group finally split. Four people decided to help take the guy with the broken ankle back to the cars that night and take him home. The others decided to finish the hike.

The decision to split the group hurt people's feelings. When the group split, those who decided to go home felt like the others were insensitive and too focused on finishing the hike. The ones who returned home late took the hurt person to urgent care. He turned out to have a bad sprain and was told to keep off it for a few days. The group members who kept on going said if everyone had pitched in together they could all have finished the hike together.

As it turned out, the weather worsened and it rained unexpectedly hard. The group members who finished the hike were soaking wet but were proud of having finished the hike. Now there's this split in the group. One group feels bad because they didn't finish the hike, but proud they pulled together and got back to town that night. The other feels justifiably proud for having endured the weather and returning home ok.

How do you heal people's feelings? How can you bring the group back together? Your group was starting to pull together before that hike, now it's fractured. You're not sure the group is going to survive. Decide what's more important: group member's feelings or the group's goal. What are you going to do?

Counsel people to help them overcome negative feelings.

Why leaders counsel

List three reasons leaders need to learn basic counseling skills.

Why leaders need to learn basic counseling skills:

Assess people's mood. As leaders grow in maturity and competence, they develop the ability to read people's behavior. They learn to assess people's moods and manners.

Identify issues. Leaders need to be able to talk to people and ask specific questions that help individuals overcome personal challenges that not only inhibit their performance but affect the entire team. Because everyone has challenges or problems from time to time.

Develop trust. Individuals grow to respect and trust effective leaders. They seek them out and ask for help.

Giving the wrong help complicates rather than reduces issues. Leaders need to know the limits of their abilities as counselors and when to refer individuals to professional help.

When to counsel

List three occasions when counseling is appropriate.

As a leader, you are responsible for helping team members grow. There are three occasions when you might need to counsel a youth.

They need help. If you think someone needs help, ask them tactfully and in private. Tell them that you sense something might be wrong. Ask him if there is anything they want to talk about. Show him know you're listening.

They need encouragement. If someone is lacking confidence, offer encouragement. Praise them for what they're doing right—and do it publicly, in front of their peers.

They need to talk. If someone wants to talk, their problem may appear unimportant to you, or it may be easily solved, but it's awfully real to the individual affected.

Do offer a listening ear when a person asks and he or she is:

Undecided. Can't or won't make a decision.

Confused. Hasn't enough facts, or more than the individual knows what to do with.

Uninformed. Lacks options, knows no way out.

Locked in (knows no alternative ways to go). Sometimes the person only thinks he's in a bind— counseling may help him find out he doesn't have a problem or help him discover the true nature of the problem.

We might also counsel with an individual when a person has made a hasty decision:

- Worried about a decision (was it right?).

- Worried about the consequences (what will happen?).

- Did not consider all the facts.

- Misinterpreted the facts.

- Did not consider all the alternatives.

Counseling may give him a "second chance" to think the matter through and decide on a reasonable course of action. It may also give the person the breathing room to allow other forces, forces they don't control, to work on and resolve the situation for them.

Getting started counseling

List three behaviors that show counseling is needed.

Behaviors that indicate the individual needs counseling include:

- The individual is upset and can't be immediately consoled.

- The individual's behavior is an ongoing challenge within the group.

- A conflict takes place that must be immediately resolved.

Is counseling needed now

Find out if the individual has to make a decision now. Sometimes they're experiencing an unwarranted sense of panic because they feel pressure to make a decision right away.

Assess the urgency. If the decision isn't actually pressing, putting off taking action can relieve the person of considerable anxiety. When you step back and leave problems alone, sometimes they work themselves out without our interference. Stepping back also helps give the individual perspective.

Once you determine there is a need for counseling, create a positive "climate" for the conversation.

Talk in private. Take the person aside—make it possible to talk in privacy and confidence.

Make them comfortable. Help him to relax and take it easy—maybe he has a hard time talking, maybe he can't stop talking. No two people are alike, so no two problems are alike. Wait and see what this person needs. Find a place to talk that's semi-private.

Give first aid

Define two parts of first aid counseling.

What is first aid counseling?

The type of counseling youth can help each other with is best called "first aid" counseling.

First aid talk. It's not therapy. It's emotional first aid. Usually the issue isn't big enough to require professional help, but if the problem cuts into the effectiveness of a group member and then *you* have a problem. Use counseling to help a group member resolve the problem if it isn't too big.

Common sense stuff. Takes away minor aches and pains. When problems come up, you usually only have a few minutes to talk. Your job is to offer on the spot first aid. If a conversation or two doesn't resolve the problem, seek out an adult. And encourage the individual to seek help at home.

Identify what hurts. What to do until the doctor arrives—helps the person tell you "where it hurts" and seek more help if needed. Suggest to the individual they seek the counsel of more knowledgeable individuals—another leader you or the individual respects, their parent, teacher, religious leader, coach, or another individual they respect.

The skills of counseling

Use these techniques for drawing a person out and encouraging them to talk. Remember, your job isn't to solve their problem for them. You task is to allow them to express themselves freely so they can make decisions in a clear and sensible fashion.

Identify the most important skill of counseling.

"Counseling" is sometimes another word for "listening."

Listening doesn't mean to sit mutely while the person spills out what's troubling them. Lacking feedback, the individual may feel ignored or unvalued. Listening means to actively attend to what the person is saying. This is "active listening."

Protect yourself

State the most important safeguard you must take as a counselor.

Avoid one-on-one contact. Under all circumstances, protect yourself and the other person against any possible hint of inappropriate behavior.

If one individual is an adult and the other is a youth, or if the two individuals are of the opposite sex, you must avoid a situation that could be misunderstood or misinterpreted.

If you're an adult working with youth, you must rigorously follow youth protection standards. Don't put yourself or the other individual at risk. You aren't a professional.

Counsel in public. If you're an adult, counsel where others can see you. If a youth wants to talk with you alone, don't meet in a private room, but find a semi-private place, like a table in a large room, or a seat outdoors.

Always give shoulder hugs. Hugs should be appropriate and initiated by the youth, not the adult. Respect the other person's boundaries. Always give a business-like "shoulder hug." Avoid a full-body hug.

Use touch appropriately. Don't touch the youth unless it's response to their need for comfort, encouragement, or affection and only if another adult is present. Don't touch a youth in any way that might give any appearance of wrongdoing. It is generally acceptable—depending on the culture—to touch a person's hand, shoulder or upper back. Avoid touching any areas generally covered by a bathing suit.

Listen actively

List at least two ways to let people know that they have your undivided attention.

- Let people know they have your full attention by practicing active listening.

- Face them and look them in the eye attentively, with compassion and love.

- Don't criticize. Listen.

- Be sure to silence or turn off your mobile device.

- Find a semi-private space to talk. Don't meet with another individual one on one in private unless you're a licensed professional.

- Really listen. Don't do anything else. Let him see that you're listening.

- Ask yourself "Do I understand what he is saying?" If you're not sure, keep listening. If you're puzzled, look puzzled—the participant probably will likely make you understand.

- Avoid asking questions that change the topic, disagreeing with the person, and questioning their perceptions or feelings.

Use non-verbal communication

List five non-verbal channels of communication.

There are five primary non-verbal channels of communication.

Posture. Sit with an open body posture. Lean forward and open your arms. Give the individual your undivided attention. Don't cross your arms or slouch.

Gestures. Keep your hands open and relaxed. Don't fidget, drum your fingers, or clench your fists.

Eye contact. Keep your eyes on his face, but don't stare. Avoid looking down at the floor which expresses disinterest or shame.

Facial expressions. Nod affirmatively, smile encouragingly, and look appropriately sober or concerned. Avoid frowning or smiling excessively.

Vocal quality. Speak directly and confidently. Don't raise your voice excessively or mumble.

Be sensitive to cultural differences. If you regularly work with individuals from different backgrounds, take time to learn about their culture and boundaries. If you aren't sure whether something is appropriate, ask.

Practice reflective listening

List three characteristics of reflective listening.

There are several ways to show a person you're listening and that you understand what they're saying.

Repeat. Occasionally repeat back what you think they said.

Verify. Ask them to confirm what you thought you heard them say.

Ask clarifying questions. "Is there anything else bothering you?" Don't overdo it! Above all, don't cross-examine or pressure him. You might offend the person and instead of calmly venting, you are the object of their anger. Be patient.

Let go. Let the other person control the pace of the conversation.

Let them talk. Don't interrupt; don't ask questions; listen until the other person stops talking. This type of listening isn't easy. Sometimes you're the subject of the conversation. Maybe they're criticizing you or something over which you have responsibility. You may feel defensive and want to interject an explanation. Don't. Listen until they're done. Then encourage them to talk more until they don't have anything to say. This allows them to "drain" all their emotions. Now they're ready to listen.

Reflect. When under stress, people's thinking in is usually muddled (otherwise they wouldn't have a problem). Reflecting what you hear back to them can help them sort out what they feel and think.

Try phrases like, "Let's see if I understand. You said that..." and give it back to him in your own words. Ask him if your understanding is correct. Asking serves two purposes: you confirm that you understand, and he can confirm that he's being heard.

Legitimize their feelings

List two behaviors that legitimize another person's feelings.

There are several behaviors that legitimize another person's feelings:

Reinforce their feelings. Say, "I can see your feelings are hurt." When you agree with what they say, it doesn't mean that you also agree with the reasons for their feelings, only that you agree that they have legitimate reason to feel as they do.

Ask him about his feelings. Feelings are legitimate and important. Encourage him to talk. "I guess that made you mad, huh?"

Agree with the person. Tell them, "I can see why you're upset," or, "If I were in your shoes, I'd feel the same way."

When individuals are troubled, they often need to talk. Sometimes talking out loud helps people to sort out their thoughts and feelings. By listening, you legitimize their worries or problems. You increase their self-esteem and their feelings of adequacy in handling the situation.

Don't take responsibility

List three reasons it's not a good idea to offer advice.

Sometimes people expect you to give them advice. They may ask, "What should I do?" Don't solve their problems for them or offer advice. This may be (probably is) what he wants—somebody to make his decision for him and relieve him of the responsibility.

Reasons it's not a good idea to offer advice include:

You take responsibility for the problem. Whatever happens now, it's your fault.

You're assuming you understand their problem. You may harm the individual by making the wrong decision—maybe you don't have all the facts yet.

People aren't usually ready to change. Offering a solution when they aren't ready to listen is a waste of time. You won't help him, because what he needs to make his own decision.

Make it clear you don't have an answer. If he asks you what he should do, boomerang it right back. "Gee, I don't know. What have you considered so far?" Giving advice is a bad ego trip. Instead, help the individual develop alternatives by offering information they may not have.

Offer encouragement

List three ways to offer encouragement and add information.

Sometimes a person who's upset may be frozen in fear and unable to see alternatives. Ask questions that stimulate thinking and encourage him. Allow the youth time to think. Wait five to ten seconds for an answer.

There are several ways to offer encouragement and add information:

Help them consider alternatives. Who have you talked to so far? Be sure it's information on which he could base his decision and not advice that makes the decision. Suggest alternative approaches to thinking about the problem and possible solutions, do so, but in as detached a manner as possible. Always suggest more than one idea, as you don't want to appear to endorse any one solution.

Ask them if they have to make a decision today. Sometimes this can help the individual relax.

Encourage them. Let him know that you have confidence in their ability to find a solution. Ask him to tell you what he decides to do. Later on, check in. Ask him how he's doing.

Talk about the worst thing that might happen. Sometimes helping a person to take an open-eyed look at reality can make a difference.

If you're unable to help the individual resolve the problem or reach a decision, it's no longer "first aid" counseling.

Perhaps the issue isn't that critical, but he needs more time than you have right now. Ask him if he's willing to set a time to talk again later. Be sure you're there!

You may also decide to refer them to others with greater expertise, or encourage them to seek help on their own. In any case, follow up so they know you care.

Norming the Group

After the group sorts out why it's together and what they need to get done, they start to build trust, unity and commitment. They are more organized about completing tasks. Now they're ready to learn about how to work together effectively.

Human relations are the most important element of a team's success. To be an effective leader, be other-oriented, empathetic, and altruistic. Look at situations and individuals from other people's point of view.

Norms aren't usually part of a group's every day conversation. They're rarely overtly considered by group members.

The norms of high-performing teams are different from what you experience every day. High performance teams usually develop their own unique set of traditions and over time.

The group may establish informal or even formal rules about how they complete tasks. They commit to early team goals. Given increased trust, they are more likely to voice their opinion.

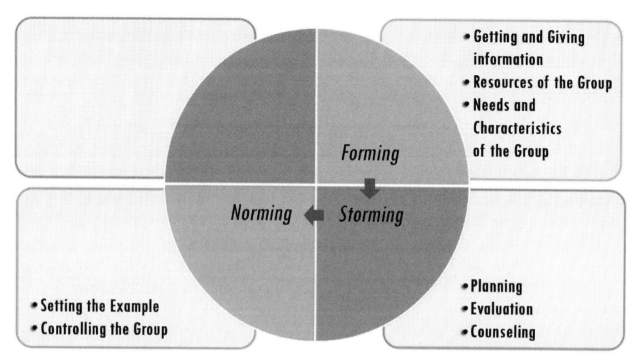

As the group starts to become effective, members need to learn about setting the example and controlling the group.

Use the next two leadership skills to help a leader to master himself so that others respect and want to follow him.

- **Setting an Example**. Every leader needs to show the way, walk to the talk, and do the right thing.

- **Controlling the Group**. To lead your team, know how to encourage and motivate team members towards achieving the team's goals.

To master these skills, learn to be sensitive to subtle behavior. It takes time and repeated practice for youth to gain a high degree of skill in them.

Your ability to put these competencies into practice makes a critical difference to your team's success. It's the difference between just getting the job done and building an effective team that helps everyone grow.

Setting the Example

About Setting the Example

We define leadership extremely simply: *keep the team together and get the job done.* Since everyone in the group can contribute to these goals, everyone is a leader. Setting the example is one way all members, no matter their position, background, or experience, can influence the group and help it achieve its goals.

If you fail to set an example that's in line with the best interests of your group and its goals, you fail the first test of a leader: walk the talk. Leadership requires action.

Example is not the main thing in influencing others. It's the only thing. —Albert Schweitzer

The idea of setting the example is easy to understand, but it's sometimes extraordinarily difficult for individuals to practice. That's because it requires self-mastery, often a leader's toughest challenge.

No competency is more important than Setting the Example. If you fail to set the example, you're doomed to failure. When your actions match your words, you build credibility and respect. People are more willing to be led by you.

Setting the Example means that your public and private selves are transparent and unified. Aligning your own thoughts and behavior with the best characteristics of leadership is often more challenging than anticipated.

Objectives

When you complete presenting the content in this chapter, learners are able to:

- List one way a leader can focus on getting what they want.

- Identify two methods a leader can help a team believe in itself.

- List two reasons why Setting the Example is not a simple competency.

- List four leadership behaviors that show an individual is Setting an Example.

- Name the most important reason a leader needs to Set an Example.

- List one rule a leader needs to follow when offering praise and giving counsel.

- List two characteristics that make a difference between a mediocre group and a winning team.

- List one way a leader overcomes failure and defeat.

- List three behaviors a leader can do to be worthy of respect.

- List two factors a leader must do over time to produce results.

- List two characteristics of having "fruit on your tree."

- List two characteristics of ethics.

- List two reasons ethics are important.

- List one difference between personal ethics and ethical leadership.

- List four attributes of an ethical leader.

- List five ways you might control a group.

Imagine

A state service organization with an interest in youth leadership heard about your Kamping for Kids program. They want to know more about your plans. They have invited members of your group to come to the state capital in January and make a presentation about your camp. The state service organization even includes members of the state legislature.

Your group is deciding who best represents the group and can most effectively talk about your goals. Someone in the group says everyone who goes should wear business clothes, like a tie or a dress. He thinks that shows you are serious. Another member complains that you don't need to dress to impress anyone. They should accept your group for who they are. A third member says that one of your group can't go because they like to swear too much. Someone reminds the group that not everyone can afford good clothes.

One of your group says that politicians are a bunch of liars and thieves. He thinks it's a waste of time to go to all the trouble to visit the capital. A girl in your group says she read a story online about the service group and it said they are a bunch of old men who don't allow women to be leaders.

You finally pick five group members to go the capital. Everyone agrees to dress sharp. You drive to the building where the state service group has its headquarters. When you're ready to park, you're a little confused and a woman wearing a red blouse in a car behind you gets impatient. She zooms around you and one of your group makes a rude gesture at her.

You park your car and find your way to the service group's building. When you exit the elevator, you see the same woman wearing the red blouse. All of a sudden you're embarrassed. You don't know if she saw the rude gesture or not. She sees you but her face doesn't give you a clue.

Your group is asked to wait before you're invited in to make your presentation. While you wait, the woman in the red blouse enters the room ahead of you. You ask the receptionist who the woman is. He says she's the Vice President. You realize the group doesn't exclude women after all.

Now your entire group is in a tight spot. A member of your group has set a bad example. They did something embarrassing and it might cost the entire group   potential support. While you all look sharp, their behavior has possibly stained everyone's reputation.

You don't know if you should pretend it didn't happen or what. Someone says you should all leave. What are your options? How do you recover? What is a mature, honest, and ethical response?

Law of mental equivalency

List one way a leader can focus on getting what they want.

An effective leader focuses his mind on what he wants and works hard to surround himself with others like himself.

Your thoughts shape your beliefs. If you believe something is true, your external world mirrors your perception. For example, if you believe that team members are constantly making mistakes, then your attention is drawn to those behaviors. If you believe team members continually give their best, you look for examples matching your expectations. As a leader, you want to focus on and pay attention to the positive in your life.

Your actions shape your thoughts

The positive association of like-minded individuals committed to common goals can yield results much greater than individuals can achieve.

Identify two methods a leader can help a team believe in itself.

Believe in people before they do. Help your team achieve success by showing them you believe in them—before they believe in themselves. An effective leader sets the example by believing in success before the team believes in itself. The successful leader inspires others to believe in themselves before they're ready.

When you start a new project, be full of enthusiasm and conviction. Sometimes you succeed in rearranging the outer world to align with your beliefs.

Action overcomes attitude. Fred Martin was a new executive in town. He soon learned that there had been a dozen people in his job during the five years before he arrived. None of them could overcome the negative challenges that were present in the position.

But he didn't let the past influence his willingness to work hard. He was full of power and energy and focused on success. His team members saw this and were influenced by his attitude. He brought in new ideas, recruited new talent, and came up with innovative programs that drew in additional clients. Unlike his predecessors, he was able to lead the team to success.

His positive attitude makes a difference.

Your thoughts and beliefs are critical to your success.

List two reasons why Setting the Example isn't a simple competency.

Setting the Example requires:

- Discipline
- Mental toughness
- Action
- Persistency and consistency

Success isn't an accident. No one becomes successful without applying themselves to the task of learning excellence. Excellence requires discipline. Discipline can't be sustained without mental toughness. Mental toughness is taking action consistent with your decisions.

The one quality which sets one man apart from another—the key which lifts one to every aspiration while others are caught up in the mire of mediocrity—is not talent, formal education nor intellectual brightness. It's self-discipline. With self-discipline, all things are possible. Without it, even the simplest goal can seem like the impossible dream. —President Theodore Roosevelt

Be consistent and persistent. Finally, success only happens when you're consistent and persistent. Nothing worth having comes to you easily or quickly. You have to set the example when it's not comfortable, convenient, or easy. Setting the Example makes a difference long after the emotion of your decision to pursue a goal is has faded.

Walk the talk

While Setting the Example appears to be an obvious concept, it isn't easy, and no competency is more important.

List four leadership behaviors that show an individual is Setting an Example.

Do your job and more. As a leader, set an example by doing what you expect others to do:

- Doing your own job well
- Go above and beyond minimum expectations
- Seek extra responsibility
- Demonstrate a positive attitude
- Follow instructions with little or no supervision

- Try your hardest
- Behave maturely

When you set the example, members of your group will yield positive results. When you walk the talk, you earn everyone's respect and find it increasingly possible to persuade the group to follow you.

Be positive

Setting the Example is where your backbone shows. If you have character, if you have integrity—that is, if who you're in public is the same person you're in private—you accomplish far more than you might imagine possible.

List two results a leader may achieve by consistently Setting an Example.

As a leader, when you consistently set an example and are a worthy leader, expect team members' respect, loyalty, and even love.

Reflect on a leader you respect and you know they set a positive example that's in alignment with their values and beliefs.

I count him braver who overcomes his desires than him who conquers his enemies;

for the hardest victory is over self. —Aristotle

It is essential that you set a positive attitude:

Team members respect integrity. They more readily follow you when your behavior is aligned with your words. Over time, this builds respect and loyalty.

Set a positive attitude. When a respected leader has a positive attitude, the group is more likely to model his behavior.

Do what you say. Group members watch more of what you do than what you say. Individuals are more influenced by your walk than your talk.

Be committed. Demonstrating a positive attitude shows your commitment to personal discipline.

Keep high standards. When your behavior matches personal and group standards, you demonstrate maturity and responsibility.

You're modeling for others how to show a positive attitude.

Set the standard

If you fail to set the example, why should you expect group members to do any better? To help keep the group together and get the job done, everything you do and say should line up with the best possible examples of leadership. When you set the example, you help facilitate the results you want as a leader.

Name the most important reason a leader needs to set an example.

People are watching. The most important reason to set an example is that wherever you are, whatever you're doing, people are watching.

At any odd second, you may be called on to take charge. As a leader, you want to be worthy of people's respect. People are taking a mental picture of you at moments you least expect—and that may well be the one image that sticks in his or her mind.

A team effort. Setting the Example is important for group members because when everyone strives to set a good example, the entire group is more successful. There are numerous ways to set an example. Whether in front of a group or sitting in a hall among thousands, you have the opportunity to act as a leader.

Follow the rules

Play league ball. If you play league ball, you play by the league rules. Listen to those in authority worthy of respect. As you gain their respect, they respect you. When you show respect for those who lead you, you earn the respect of those who follow you.

Ask questions. If you don't understand the rules, ask questions until you do. If the rules don't make sense, work on changing the rules. If you don't like the rules, talk to your leaders. Don't complain to your peers or those you lead. You'll lose their respect.

Praise in public, counsel in private

List one rule a leader needs to follow when offering praise and giving counsel.

Praise in public. Share credit liberally and publicly with those responsible for your success. By lifting them up, you lift yourself up in their eyes. You demonstrate respect for their contribution and they offer you respect in return.

Encouragement is oxygen for the soul. It takes very little effort to give it, but the return in others is huge. —John C. Maxwell

---

Counsel in private. When you must counsel with someone, do so privately, out of earshot of others.

Pass negative up, not down. Don't criticize your leaders to those you lead. You lose their respect. Reserve your complaints, criticisms, and concerns for those who lead you.

I don't gripe to you, Reiben. I'm a captain. There's a chain of command. Gripes go up, not down. Always up. You gripe to me, I gripe to my superior officer, so on, so on, and so on. I don't gripe to you. I don't gripe in front of you. You should know that as a Ranger. —Captain Miller, "Saving Private Ryan" (1998)

Give more than required

On time means be early. Start with the basics: show up, and show up on time. "On time" means 10 minutes early. Participate to the best of your ability. Contribute to discussions and look for ways to be helpful. When the meeting or event ends, don't be in a rush to leave. Look for opportunities to connect with individuals and build relationships. You can also sometimes obtain new information and insights in "the meeting after the meeting."

Don't give up. But successful people take the extra step of showing up when others have given up. They remain persistent and committed to their vision beyond reason, when rational thought and convention would require them to quit.

Success is the sum of small efforts, repeated day in and day out... —Robert Collier

Following instructions isn't enough. Doing exactly what you have been given to do doesn't produce success, only mediocrity.

List two characteristics that make a difference between a mediocre group and a winning team.

Give 100%. A winning team gives 100% and does the best job it can. An excellent leader stays true to his vision, seizes opportunities, and takes calculated risks. A mediocre leader does the minimum and avoids risk-taking.

Do your best. Don't wait for instruction, but seize the initiative. When needed, step outside your immediate lines of authority and take a chance. A leader who shares in the risks and hardships is admired by those who follow him. Persistence and consistency can make up for shortfalls in other areas.

Stand up for what's right. Everyone admires individuals who are willing to stand up for what they believe. Steadfast commitment to visions and goals inspires others and draws them to you. When others can see and feel your excitement and passion, you ignite in them a desire to share that energy.

Be out front

Lead from the front. Don't ask others to do anything you aren't willing to do yourself. When you lead from the front, it means you also give first, sacrifice first, and pay the price before everyone else.

Always remember the power of your example and positive influence when you lead from the front.

Take the initiative

Don't wait for others to act. When an opportunity presents itself, seize the moment to move forward. If you stumble, don't stop. Keep moving forward.

List one way a leader overcomes failure and defeat.

Be persistent. When facing failure and defeat, don't give up. Keep on trying. Even though you may fail at times, you earn your team members' respect. You're not a failure as long as you keep getting up.

When something doesn't work, don't stop trying. Look for another way. Seek other people's input. Be steadfast and loyal to your own vision. Stick with it even when you don't see progress. Use the "slight edge" to your advantage, knowing that the little bit of progress you make each day, with the advantage of time, gets you closer to your goal.

Don't procrastinate. Focus on what needs to be done without putting it off until forced to do it. Seize the day. Nothing ever comes to those who wait. Ask for what you want. Look for opportunities to help.

Success seems to be largely a matter of hanging on after others have let go.
—William Feather

Law of respect

List three behaviors a leader can do to be worthy of respect.

Show good judgment. Don't clown around, disturb others, or goof off.

Watch your language. Don't use crude or offensive language at any time. Don't joke with someone you don't know. Their sense of humor may be entirely different than yours. Let your behavior be marked by maturity, respect, and dignity.

Give respect first. Leaders act as if they deserve the respect of those they serve. Give respect before you expect it from others. Nobody who demands respect ever gets it, except as lip service, while they're around.

Show self-respect. Show respect for your body and avoid excessive piercings, tattoos, and other body art. For women, avoid multiple earrings. Sure, it's your right to do whatever you want to your body. But is it worth the cost of a job you really need? You only have one chance to make a first impression. Make sure it's a good one.

Dress for success

Life is unfair. Like it or not, people judge you based on what your wear and how you look.

Dress appropriately. Dress in a manner befitting the occasion, group, and task. If you're attending a leadership meeting, dress like a leader. If attending leadership development, wear clothing appropriate to the activity. Avoid clothing that would potentially distract others.

Neatness counts. Keep your person and personal appearance clean. Keep your hair manageable and neat—all affect others' perception of the example you set. Strive to keep your personal areas that you're responsible for tidy and organized.

Women. For women, that means avoiding cleavage, midriff-baring T-shirts, clingy tight tops, and short skirts or short-shorts. Don't give anyone the opportunity to think of you in inappropriate ways or distract them from the task at hand.

Men. For men, that means pants that you wear around your waist, not your thighs. Men should also dress neatly and conservatively. Your clothes should fit well and enable you to act in a manner befitting the occasion. If you have to tug clothing into place, then it probably doesn't fit you or the occasion. Leave the Hawaiian shirts, flip-flops, and sandals for the beach.

Know your job

Keep the "big picture" in mind along with the nitty-gritty. Find out what is expected by those you lead and by those you report to. Be personally proficient in outdoor and leadership skills. You ought to be a good resource for anybody in your group, but not necessarily the best at everything.

Don't wind up doing everything because you know how—stick to your job as leader. Know your group members' strengths and weaknesses. Know how to back each member up and make everyone look good.

Law of attraction

Your mind becomes attuned to give attention to whatever you spend the majority of your time thinking about. As an effective leader, you want to attract individuals who mirror your positive capabilities, hopes and aspirations.

List two attitudes a leader needs to produce results.

Focus on the positive. "Like attracts like." The law of attraction is based on the belief that positive thoughts bring about positive results. In a relationship, if you focus on what you dislike about a person, you experience the negative attributes of their personality. If you focus on the person's good qualities, you experience more of their positive attributes.

Likewise, if you spend time wallowing in regret over past mistakes, or anticipating future fears, you experience more negativity.

Watch your thoughts, they become words;

watch your words, they become actions;

watch your actions, they become habits;

watch your habits, they become character;

watch your character, for it becomes your destiny

—Frank Outlaw, late president of Bi-Lo Stores

Expect good results. Nature can educate a willing leader much about leadership. In nature, most seeds don't germinate. When they grow, it takes time to reap a harvest. The more seeds you plant, the greater your harvest.

Visualize what you want. Based on the law of attraction, visualizes clearly and in detail what they want to achieve, and focuses upon that image, that they set in motion through the law of attraction a chain of events that eventually culminates in the materialization of that vision.

Law of the fruit

If you want to know how successful someone is, look at the fruit on their tree.

List two characteristics of having "fruit on your tree."

You harvest what you sow. In nature, you can't plant apples and expect to harvest watermelons. It's the same way with people. When you're looking at the "fruit on someone's tree," you're quickly evaluating if they're someone you want to hang with. A person's life reflects the consequences of their actions.

If you sow roses in the form of confidence, compliments, and uplifting conversation in people around you, you get—big surprise here—more roses. Conversely, if you gossip, belittle, condemn and criticize others, you're planting thorns, and that's what you harvest. Look at the fruit on the tree of those around you.

Look at your own fruit. What are you harvesting in your life? If you're not happy with your life, then make changes.

Choose your association

Choose your association wisely. One of the most important decisions you make in life is who you hang with. To be an effective leader, carefully choose who you spend your time with. Because the more time you spend around others, the more likely you are to adopt their attitudes, values, and beliefs.

Even when you set a positive example, you can't expect that every team member instantly catches on and follows your lead.

Set an example

Setting an example requires patience. You must invest time into the team because they can't always immediately follow your example. Time is necessary to build relationships with team members, to establish trust and mutual respect. As you persist with your leadership practice, you begin to produce fruit—to achieve success—with a few team members more ready and willing than others.

Team members follow you. Members of other teams see the positive changes in those who are following you. They want that for themselves. They want to belong to the winning team beginning to form within the larger group.

Your character shapes the team's character. As a leader, followers do what you do. If you're internally confused, the team is externally confused. When you're generous with praise, team members are confident and full of esteem. As you show your confidence and respect for team members, they respond in kind to you.

Individuals rise to your level of expectation. When you lift team members' expectations of themselves, they respect you. As you show members that you care for them as individuals, they respond to your direction for them as a team.

Law of the tongue

Think about your something you did well. How did you begin? When you reflect on how you started, you find that it started in your thoughts. And from there you began to talk about it—you used your tongue. All of our behavior originates in our minds. It's imperative that you learn how to control your thoughts, and in turn, what you say.

Identify one way your thoughts can mislead you.

One way your thoughts can mislead you is when you make decisions based on faulty information.

Thoughts create beliefs. Your thoughts represent your beliefs. Thoughts are also merely ideas that your inner self gives voice to, rising out of your mind to a conscious level. Having a thought doesn't make it either a fact or a truth.

For example, during a conversation with someone, you may "hear" something the other person didn't actually say. You may have unknowingly misunderstood them; you may have inaccurately interpreted their body language; you might have projected your thoughts and feelings onto them. And you reach a conclusion based on false evidence. As powerful as your thoughts feel, as real as they feel, they aren't necessarily accurate or true.

You will never go higher than your thinking. —*Benjamin Disraeli*

Charge your mind

Identify the most effective way to change how you think.

Choose positive self-talk. You know self-talk: it's that semi-constant "internal monologue" going on in your mind; it's the little voice inside your head that, when you try something hard, says, "Are you sure you can do this? Your friends don't do stuff like this. This isn't a good idea." Even though your thoughts might often be biased or incorrect, you tend to assume that they're facts. Self-talk often tends to be negative, and sometimes its plain wrong.

Self-talk has a huge impact on how you feel. Unfortunately, we tend to think that our feelings are real, even if they are based on false information.

Change starts within. People often make the mistake of thinking change begins by changing the environment around them. They think changing external circumstances changes their problems. This is like painting the leaves of your dying plant green instead of watering and fertilizing it. Instead, modify the beliefs that created your circumstances.

Focus on the positive. Setting the example begins in your own mind. It's widely accepted that when you focus on what you read or hear, you increase concentration and retention. The same is true when you focus on your thoughts. You want to be sure you're focusing on positive thoughts, not negative ones.

What the mind of man can conceive and believe, it can achieve. —Napoleon Hill

The more you concentrate on a thought, the more time and energy you devote to it, the more real it is to your mind. As a leader, your first task is to control your thoughts, to eliminate "weedy" thoughts that don't contribute to your own or the team's success.

Unsuccessful people dwell on the negative, spend their time and energy complaining, and worry about unimportant issues. Their negativity costs them time and energy that they could use to focus on their goals.

Everyone can program their mind. During the 1970s, John Grinder and Richard Bandler defined the field of neuron-linguistic programming while at the University of California at Santa Cruz. They had witnessed how people with similar educational, training, experience, and background achieved widely dissimilar results.

The two men conducted research to identify what effective people did that made a difference. They identified patterns of thinking that helped people be more successful. They concluded that the brain can learn healthy patterns and behaviors that produce positive physical and emotional effects. Their basic premise is that the thoughts and words you use reflect our inner, subconscious perceptions. How you talk about your inner self becomes a self-fulfilling prophecy.

The thought manifests as the word,

The word manifests as the deed,

The deed develops into habit,

And the habit hardens into character.

So watch the thought and its way with care,

And let it spring from love

Born out of concern for all beings. —*Sri Dhammananda*

Remodel your self-talk

Therapists who practice neuron-linguistic programming help individuals to "remodel" their thoughts and mental associations, modifying their preconceived beliefs. But you don't need a therapist to do this. Here's how to do it yourself.

Setting the Example begins with changing your thinking.

Learn a new self-talk. The path to controlling your thoughts is to learn a new self-talk language. Practically speaking, this means recognizing and interrupting the typically negative stream of thoughts coming out of your brain. Then replace that stream with specific ideas that are in agreement with your goals.

Change what you think, say, and see. Remodel your thoughts, what you say, and what you see. You want to adjust what you think, what you expect, and what you speak. This is the art of self-talk. To change your future, you must change your present.

Your mind is conditioned to believe that what you think and say. When you replace your uncontrolled internal monologue with self-talk that is linked with your goals, your self-talk influences what you say, which in turn influences what you see and do.

Give your brain new input. If you want to change how you think, give your brain as much new input as possible. Use self-talk—both words and pictures—to change your thinking. Successful people visualize their goals and take action to make them happen.

One of the failures of traditional education is that it relies primarily on two senses: hearing and seeing. Research has found that people learn more effectively when more of their senses are involved.

Use visual imagery

Using pictures is especially important. Roughly one-third of the human brain is dedicated to processing visual imagery. If you want to control your thinking, feed your brain images that support what you want it to think.

Interviews with successful people have proven that one of the essential elements of their accomplishments is that they visualize success. Visual imagery is usually the most important psychological tool for an athlete.

Visualization improves performance. Research has proven that visualization improves the quality of athletes' physical movement, their power of concentration, ability to focus, confidence, and self-composure. Mental imagery enables athletes to review their performance and prepare their mind and body for the specific movements necessary for peak performance.

During their actual performance, it has been found to reduce stress and anxiety. It may also increase energy levels and even reduce injuries.

Wayne Rooney is a striker for Manchester United, the highest ranked soccer club in England. Rooney habitually asks the club's uniform man the color uniform the team is wearing the next day. Before every match, Rooney visualizes his team's victory to the smallest detail, including what they're wearing, for one special purpose: to enhance the completeness of his psychological preparation.

Pathways in your brain. Scientists theorize that the reason visual imagery works is that when you imagine yourself performing at your optimal level, you're creating neural patterns in your brain, as if you had physically performed the action.

Prove it. Demonstrate this for yourself. Stand with your arms out at shoulder height. Rotate them like a helicopter as far as you possibly can and note your progress before returning your arms to your sides. Now close your eyes for two minutes and imagine going through the motions again. See yourself rotating your arms as far as possible and the comfort and ease you feel as you do this. Do this in your mind several times. Then open your eyes and repeat the physical exercise. Surprisingly, you're able to rotate your arms easier and farther than you did the first time. (Stop reading and actually do it. You'll be amazed!)

Prepare your mind. Everyone understands that humans can learn to react instinctively to a variety of situations. Soldiers train again and again so that when they face a real battle they're able to react without thinking.

The subconscious mind can perceive emotions and behaviors the conscious mind can't and can react more quickly than the conscious mind.

Rehearse your success. In the same way that athletes and soldiers mentally rehearse their victory, rehearse yours. Start imagining it as if it's already true. Self-talk is your Olympic leadership education.

Use words

The practice of self-talk isn't on the list of subjects taught in high school or even college. You might find a self-help consultant in your area who offers a workshop, if you're lucky and if you have a couple hundred dollars handy.

You may find at first that self-talk feels foreign or even phony. The more often you practice self-talk, the more real and comfortable it becomes.

Write your goals down. Visualize what you want. Think of words and images that emotionally capture what you want to achieve.

Be specific. Describe your vision and goals in specific terms. Then write them in the present tense describe what you want.

Speak affirmatively. Use strong, declarative, affirmative language. Say "I am", not "I'll try."

Use images. Find pictures that evoke what you want to achieve. For example, if you want to lose weight, find pictures of clothing that you would like to reward yourself with when you reach your goal. Put pictures where you can see them. Then move them from time to time so you won't begin to ignore them.

Write down what you want. Populate your life with copies of your written affirmations. For example, make a copy and tape it to your bathroom or bedroom mirror. Put one in zip lock bag in your shower. Tape another copy to your car steering wheel or visor. Put another copy in your bill fold so every time you open your wallet, you can view your affirmation.

Repeat your affirmations. Repeat your affirmations several times daily, preferably out loud, with confidence and conviction. Start in the shower, the bathroom, or another private space. It can feel awkward and silly at first because you're unused to this way of thinking. But persevere and remain consistent. And every day, do something, however small that advances you towards your goal.

For example, if your goal is to lose weight, you might write statements like the following:

- I am losing weight every day.
- I enjoy eating fruits and vegetables.
- I love losing weight.

- I am learning to eat healthy.

- I am changing the way I eat.

- I am healthier every day.

- I do something every day, no matter how small, to move me towards my goal.

- You can't see it yet, but my body is looking skinnier and firmer every day.

- I love taking the stairs instead of the elevator.

- I like feeling my faster heart rate when I exercise.

Law of attitude

As you improve your skill at self-talk, you change your attitude. Self-talk and attitudes are inextricably linked.

Be accountable. You can't control your environment and circumstances. But you control how you perceive what you experience and how you respond. One of the key approaches to mastering your attitude is developing an attitude of accountability. This means that you take responsibility to a degree for everything that happens to you. You decide to stop blaming others, that you aren't a victim, and are in fact responsible for your life.

Having a willingness to control your attitude allows you to decide how you behave. Choose whether to hold on to regrets and resentments, or whether to forgive and forget. Decide whether you want contention or peace in your life.

Cultivate a positive attitude. One way to set a positive example is to consciously cultivate a positive attitude. Show that you're excited, confident, and enthusiastic about your goals.

Any fact facing us is not as important as our attitude toward it, for that determines our success or failure. The way you thing about a fact may defeat you before you ever do anything about it. You are overcome by the fact because you think you are.
—*Norman Vincent Peale*

If you don't feel confident, fake it until the feeling returns. If necessary, pump yourself up. Create enthusiasm by acting enthusiastically. If you don't believe this, try doing 20 jumping jacks while shouting enthusiastically about your goals.

Be the winning coach. When problem-solving, focus on solutions and issues, not problems and people. Decide that you're making a difference and that you're part of a winning team. Every winning team has a coach with a winning attitude.

Obsession is a good thing. Focus on your goals relentlessly. Eliminate distractions and negative thoughts. When you do, your attitude gets noticed. People adopt your opinions because they want to be like you. They follow you because they value your goals. Make sure that your attitude is the best possible.

Talent is not enough

The world is full of talented individuals who fail as leaders. The difference between successful and unsuccessful people is not talent; it's a willingness to work harder than your peers. People have excuses about why they aren't successful. Excuses are easy. Developing a winning attitude, despite obstacles and setbacks, is hard.

If you want to be successful, you must demonstrate to others that you're willing to go the extra mile to finish your job. This requires consistent effort and self-discipline. To stand out from the crowd, an effective leader strives to give 100% when it's needed most. He looks for opportunities to go out of his way to serve others, especially when it's not expected.

A racehorse that consistently runs just a second faster than another horse is worth millions of dollars more. Be willing to give that extra effort that separates the winner from the one in second place. —H. Jackson Brown, "Life's Little Instruction Book"

An effective leader doesn't show up on time and leave as soon as the job is done. When given an assignment, they look beyond the specific task for other contributions they can make. They don't do the minimum. J.C. Penny was asked the key to his success. "Work half days, and it doesn't matter if it's the first half or the second half."

Match your inside and outside

Setting the Example is the "internal" component of Controlling the Group. When you earn your group's respect, when you act mature, show initiative, and demonstrate an attitude for getting business done, they are likely to follow you. The group works together better and gets more done.

I'd rather see a sermon
than hear one—any day.

I'd rather one should walk with me,
than merely show the way.

The eye's a better pupil
and more willing than the ear;
Fine counsel is confusing,
but example is always clear.

The best of all the preachers
are the men who live their creeds,
For, to see the good in action
is what everybody needs.

I can say, I'll learn how to do it
if you'll let me see it done;
I can watch you hand in action
through your tongue too fast may run.

Although the lectures you deliver
may be very wise and true,
I'd rather learn my lesson by
observing what you do;

For I may misunderstand you
and the fine advice you give,
But it's no misunderstanding
how you act and how you live.

—Edgar A. Guest

Motivate and inspire others

Most people think that people need to be motivated. *Wrong.*

People are already motivated. Adults are motivated because they need food, money, or a new television. Convention centers and hotel ball rooms are full every weekend across the United States with adults who want to feel motivated. Attendees spend one or two days getting filled with apparently powerful motivational techniques, with clues to unlocking their unlimited potential.

Motivation is a like your first bungee jump. You are excited, energized and enthusiastic for a while, but all you're left with is the memory and maybe a video.

Teens are wired a little differently. You're motivated by a desire to belong, to have a say about situations that affect you, to assume real responsibility, to make a real contribution, to learn about things that involve you, and to have fun.

But to reach beyond the necessities of life for something greater, people need to be inspired.

Motivate them. Motivation is good because it opens you to growth. But motivation is external and temporary.

The good news is that these speakers encourage people to think. They stimulate attendees, encourage new ways of thinking, and challenge them to set new goals. External motivation may wake you up, but it won't keep you awake. Once the emotion of the event fades, so does the motivation.

The whole idea of motivation is a trap. Forget motivation. Just do it. Exercise, lose weight, test your blood sugar, or whatever. Do it without motivation. And then, guess what? After you start doing the thing, that's when the motivation comes and makes it easy for you to keep on doing it. — John C. Maxwell

Inspire them. Inspiration comes from within and is lasting. It gives people a reason to grow. You want to give them the tools they need to change and grow, tools that help them find a reason to succeed. But the most important gift you give people is to help them find their why. Why do they want to succeed? What is their dream?

Lift members' expectations

As a leader, establish high standards for what you expect from your team members. Individuals tend to rise to the level of expectations communicated to them.

Belief is essential. In 1968, Robert Rosenthal and Lenore Jacobson conducted an influential study in a San Francisco elementary school. They told a selected team of teachers that their students had a higher learning potential than other students.

At the end of the year, the students in those classes had higher academic achievement than students that did not take part in the study. In actuality, there was no difference between the students in the selected classes and the rest of the school. It was the teacher's expectations or attitude that made the difference.

Share team leadership

While leadership is shared by all members of a team, effective teams are typically led by a formally designated individual who gives the team direction and focus.

Depending on the job and the team, a formal leader chooses different ways to interact with the team and team members. One of the essential responsibilities of the selected leader is to share leadership with other members of the team.

Sharing Leadership is about two types of leadership behavior:

Informal. How informal leaders within the team assume leadership roles and responsibilities

Formal. How the formal leader uses specific behaviors to help the team accomplish its goals and keep the team together.

An especially effective leader "clones" himself by mentoring and developing other leaders.

An effective leader helps a team achieve its goals. When leadership is distributed to team members, the entire organization is more able and ready to respond to a variety of circumstances which a single leader can't anticipate. An effective team can accomplish jobs greater than one person alone can handle. This is an essential element of our society's success today. Our society has reached a previously unattainable level of productivity.

Law of ethical leadership

There have been a large number of public and business leaders who have made poor ethical decisions. A few leaders don't consider—or perhaps don't care—how their decisions affect others. Their first priority is profit--for them and their businesses. They avoid ethical responsibility and make decisions based on their own selfish wants.

An ethical leader puts the needs of his team and community ahead of self-interest. He bases his decisions on the Golden Rule.

Do unto others as you would have them do unto you.

The underlying principle of the Golden Rule is that we strive to treat others as we would like to be treated our self—with tolerance, consideration, patience, kindness, compassion, and similar good virtues.

List two characteristics of ethics.

Ethics are based on our values. Ethics are moral principles or standards that guide our conduct. They're based on our values.

- Values are core beliefs like duty, honesty, honor, and integrity. They influence our attitudes and motivate our actions.

- Values guide you to choose between right and wrong. They form the foundation for both individual and team ethics.

List two reasons ethics are important.

- Ethics are necessary because they provide leaders with a foundation and moral compass.

- Without properly grounded ethics based in values that benefit community and society, you may make decisions that hurt and hinder yourself and others.

List one difference between personal ethics and ethical leadership.

There isn't any. You can't apply one set of rules to your personal life and a second set of rules to your team. That isn't ethical.

Make ethical behavior a priority. As an ethical leader, your priority is to put people before the organizational.

Personal vs. organizational ethics. There may be differences between an individual's ethics and an organization's ethics. **Example**: A police officer may be obligated to enforce laws that he doesn't agree with.

Every individual has to choose how to apply ethics. Be informed and knowledgeable about the organization's ethics and values and why they exist. Understand the consequences if you choose to disobey the organization's ethics.

Some organizations develop a "code of ethics" to reinforce what's expected of members and employees.

As a citizen, you may object to certain laws of the land. You have a choice to obey them anyhow, or to disobey them and risk consequences. Martin Luther King was willing to go to jail to fight unjust laws that were eventually overruled, in part because of his ethical leadership.

The U.S. Army, in 1986, had as the theme for the year "values," and listed four organizational values—loyalty, duty, selfless service, and integrity—and four individual values: commitment, competence, candor, and courage.

List four attributes of an ethical leader.

Demonstrate character. An ethical leader acts with integrity, honor, truthfulness, fairness, and respect. They put the interests of those they lead ahead of their own. These attributes are generally described as *character*. Character is the combination of personal qualities that make each person unique.

The world is full of bad examples of ethical behavior.

- Multi-millionaires who accept huge bonuses when their companies are failing and accepting citizen's tax dollars to keep them alive.

- Fast food companies that market food that is unhealthy and contributes to an obesity epidemic among youth.

- Television shows that pay the winner for stabbing fellow castaways in the back.

- A president who lies about having sex in the White House with an intern.

As teens, youth may witness poor ethics among their peers. For example:

- Students who copy information from the Internet and with little alteration add it to a report they're writing.

- Students who ask to copy your homework.

- Friends who cancel plans with you because something more interesting came along.

Ethical behavior is becoming increasingly uncommon.

A few organizations are attempting to counteract this loss of character. The Josephson Institute has had great success promoting The Six Pillars of Character: *Respect, Responsibility, Fairness, Caring,* and *Citizenship.*

Integrity without knowledge is weak and useless, and knowledge without integrity is dangerous and dreadful. —Samuel Johnson

If these sound familiar, it's because the Boy Scouts of America has had its own pillars of character in place since 1910. They're called the Boy Scout Law.

A Scout is trustworthy, loyal, helpful, friendly, courteous, kind, obedient, cheerful, thrifty, brave, clean, and reverent.

A few individuals in positions of authority gain considerable power, but without ethics to guide them, can lose their way and abuse their responsibility. CEO Kenneth L. Lay led energy giant Enron during a critical time when our country's electrical distribution system was liberalized to increase economic competitiveness. He and CFO Andrew Fastow teamed up with executives at Arthur Anderson to manipulate the energy market.

They amassed great personal wealth. But when their unethical and illegal behavior was revealed, both companies collapsed. On the last business day before filing for bankruptcy, Enron executives awarded themselves $55 million in cash bonuses on top of another $50 million in bonuses only weeks earlier. Shareholders lost $74 billion dollars, of which $40 to $45 billion was attributed to fraud.

As leaders in your school, community, and organization, you commit to lead ethical lives. As leaders of highly effective teams, you're in the forefront of learning and practicing ethical leadership.

Controlling the Group

About Controlling the Group

Controlling the Group helps leaders to discover team members' needs and work to align them with the group's goals and objectives. In traditional corporate management, companies seek to motivate employees by recognizing and rewarding them for achieving goals.

When individuals think about controlling the group, the first thing that usually comes to mind are restrictions placed by others limiting what they can do. Managers think about the rewards they offer employees for achieving goals. The reward is usually thought to offer the employee *motivation* to succeed.

Research into behavior shows that there are two types of motivation: external or *extrinsic*, and internal or *intrinsic*.

Motivation: The root meaning of *motivation* is to move. Motivation is usually based on an external or an intrinsic reward, something the person hopes to receive from the experience.

Inspiration: The root meaning of *inspiration* is to inspire, or breathe in. Inspiration means to infuse an idea into a person's mind, to communicate with their spirit, or to affect a person emotionally.

Objectives

When you complete presenting the content in this chapter, learners are able to:

- List five ways you might control a group
- List the primary purpose of groups.
- List two characteristics of Controlling the Group.
- Identify the person primarily responsible for Controlling the Group.
- List three factors a leader can't always control.
- List three attitudes of effective groups.
- List two key factors that influence a leader's ability to help his group succeed.
- List two reasons why it's a good idea to give correction before the task is completed.
- List at least two occasions when it's appropriate to praise individual success.
- State the maximum physical distance a leader can have and still effectively control the group.
- List three behaviors that help team members develop respect for you.
- List at least two ways a leader builds trust with the group.
- List at least two ways a leader reinforces what's right.

Imagine

After your group presented your idea for Kamping for Kids to a representative from the state service organization a month and a half ago, you thought you'd failed. But last week your faculty advisor received an email announcing that your group had been given you the money, with a couple of additional requirements.

Everyone in the group is excited. Everyone is pulling together now. They are wearing their polo shirts with your group's logo on it to school with pride. The local newspaper ran another story about your receiving the grant. Your team's big idea, what appeared impossible when you first thought of it, now looks like it might happen after all.

Everyone is tossing out ideas for different activities to help communicate your goals to participants. The meeting is turning chaotic.

How do you keep the team focused on the task? How do you refine all of the ideas? A few members are way off target and now that everyone's charged up, you don't want to hurt people's feelings. How do you identify the ones that work? How do you maintain their enthusiasm and momentum and also persuade them to focus on specifics?

You need to control the group.

Define the group's purpose

List five ways you might control a group.

Mix members up. Sometimes individuals aren't working together. Give them tasks that give them distance.

Delegate tasks. You know your team and what individual members are able to do. Delegate tasks to **individuals** that take advantage of their skills and abilities.

Recognize success. When someone is doing well, let them know. Even more importantly, recognize them in front of the group.

Communicate clearly. Make sure everyone understands what's expected of them, the rules and procedures, the goals and the task at hand.

Keep people on task. Sometimes people wander off-task or show up late. Let them know that you and their team is relying on them. Give them pointers to improve their behavior. And always offer feedback in private.

List the primary purpose of groups.

Groups exist for a purpose. People join an organization because they believe in its goals. But the group isn't successful unless members prosper. The group exists to both accomplish its goals and enhance its member's lives.

List two characteristics of Controlling the Group.

As a leader seeking to control the group, you're helping the group maintain a balance between keeping the team together and getting the job done.

Be the throttle. Controlling the Group is like having your hand on the throttle to the group's engine. Your job as the leader is to help the group move forward at optimum speed. As the leader, you influence the group and strive to maintain an optimum balance between the group's purpose or task and keeping team members motivated and happy.

Identify the person primarily responsible for Controlling the Group.

The Leader finds a Balance. Controlling the Group is your responsibility. You're in the best position to understand the group dynamics and to help the group achieve a balanced approach to both completing the task and keeping the team together.

Control what you can

List three factors a leader can't always control.

As a leader, you sometimes have to cope with factors that you don't have any control over:

Physical environment. You may have limited control over the location, environment, or weather.

Project. You may have been assigned a project and you don't have any say in the scope.

Time. You may be given time constraints that you have to live within.

People. You may need to work with another group or individuals you don't know or who are difficult to interact with.

You have the most influence over the team itself. Identifying the most appropriate style of leadership for a team depends on a variety of variables. Your team may be more or less ready to work together, and have a few or all of the required skills.

Over a period of time, your team needs varying amounts and types of assistance to achieve its goals. A few people need more assistance with job-related issues while others require help with team-focused needs.

Have an attitude

List three attitudes of effective individuals.

Effective individuals are:

- Self-directed.
- Inspired.
- Committed for the long-term.

- Ambitious.
- Possess self-control.

Help the group succeed

List two key factors that influence a leader's ability to help his group succeed.

There are two forces affecting a leader's ability to shepherd his group to success:

- His own skill.
- The group's readiness and ability.

Assert control

You may need to assert control in a variety of situations. One of the most effective ways to exert control, or influence behavior, is to recognize and reward the behaviors wanted. This has been shown to be much more effective than correcting bad or ineffective behaviors.

Recognize good work

Recognize each individual's contributions to group goals as soon as practical, even while they're still engaged in the task. Everyone appreciates receiving positive, timely feedback.

List two reasons why it's a good idea to give correction before the task is completed.

Giving correction before the task is completed is more effective.

Avoids rework. Team members avoid rework, fixing what's wrong while in progress.

Increases success. The task is accomplished more quickly and team members experience more success.

List at least two occasions when it's appropriate to praise individual success.

It is always appropriate to offer praise, both in public and in private.

People always appreciate recognition. Take every opportunity to praise individuals, offer an encouraging word, and recognize performance. Praise is particularly effective when you give it publicly.

When someone does something right, give positive, sincere feedback. Don't do it if it's not from your heart—your phoniness shows right through and you lose respect. But do it sincerely and you not only earn their respect, you gain their loyalty.

Be present

State the maximum physical distance a leader can have and still effectively control the group.

No maximum distance. There is no maximum distance because Controlling the Group doesn't depend on how close you are. It depends on your relationship with team members.

You don't have to be physically present to control the group, because a leader influences people both directly and indirectly. Team members support team goals because of their commitment and loyalty to the organization and based on their relationship with you.

The leader's influence. You are not the only individual exercising influence on the group. Other members reinforce one another behavior according to an unwritten group code (norms). Group members, knowing the group's purpose, may correct one another.

The group usually allows the leader to exert primary control. You help members retain a sense of unity while focusing the group on completing the task they're responsible for.

Show respect, get respect

List three behaviors that help team members develop respect for you.

You create respect when you:

- Don't find fault with others
- Value other people's opinions
- Recognize individual success
- Provide consistent and clear communication
- Tolerate differences.

Give and build respect

Mutual respect. The relationship between team members and the leader is built over time. It's based on mutual respect and two-way support, a shared vision, common beliefs, and trust.

Respect isn't related to someone's "worthiness" or their importance to the organization. Respect means you don't pass judgment on other's contributions. Respect is the foundation for building an effective relationship between you and your team members.

Don't judge others, but use your judgment.

Use your judgment. There are times in your life when it's important to distinguish between someone who innocently screws up and someone who purposefully or repeatedly makes mistakes. Don't pass judgment on the first person, and stop expecting results from the second guy. Use your judgment about giving him further responsibilities.

You may want to offer correction to the second guy and give him another chance. Or you may want to stop giving him important work to do until he shows he's ready to sincerely try again.

The final test of a leader is that he leaves behind him in other men the conviction and will to carry on. — *Walter Lippmann*

Demonstrate trust

List at least two ways a leader builds trust with the group.

Build trust by:

Giving responsibility. Allow team members to assume responsibility for important tasks. Team members appreciate the confidence you show in them when you don't stand right over their shoulders. Give credit where credit is due and shoulders responsibility when something goes wrong.

When something does go wrong, don't wait long to step in and make course corrections. Call a halt if appropriate and bring the group together. Guide the team through a quick evaluation session. Give input where needed and let them return to the task at hand.

Acknowledging individual contributions. Acknowledge how individuals specifically contributed to the team's success.

Taking an interest in team members. Show respect for them as individuals by greeting them by name. As you learn about their personal life, take a moment now and again to ask personal (not prying) questions. Be sincere when you show your interest. Your team members know the difference.

One way you build trust is by allowing someone to try again after they make a mistake. Test pilot Bob Hoover took off one day in his Shrike Commander on his way to Los Angeles when the plane's two engines suddenly died. Hoover safely crash landed the multi-passenger plane but it was badly damaged. Fortunately, neither he nor his two passengers were hurt.

Wondering about the cause of the sudden engine failure, he smelled the fuel. Instead of gasoline, he smelled jet fuel. A member of the ground crew had mistaken the piston engine plane for a turboprop and mis-fueled it.

When he returned to the air field, Bob Hoover walked over to the mechanic responsible for fueling the airplane. The young man knew he'd caused the crash, destroying an expensive aircraft and nearly killing three people. Hoover didn't raise his voice or even criticize him. Instead, he put his arm around the man's shoulder and, according to his autobiography, said:

"There isn't a man alive who hasn't made a mistake. But I'm positive you'll never make this mistake again. That's why I want to make sure that you're the only one to refuel my plane tomorrow. I won't let anyone else on the field touch it."

Reinforce what's right

List at least two ways a leader reinforces what's right.

Reinforce what's right by:

- Offering encouragement and praise.
- Lending assistance as required.
- Using a positive and confident manner and tone.
- Avoiding threats and yelling.
- Giving reasons for extra effort.
- Praising individual efforts in public.
- Counseling individuals and provide correction in private.

To be an effective leader, take time to let everyone know how their contribution is making a difference, no matter how slight.

Reinforcing positive behavior alone is more effective than correcting negative behavior alone. —Unknown

When working with more than one group, a leader needs to concentrate on the group doing the most important job, unless all jobs are equal. In that case, watch the largest group, with the greatest potential for error, most closely. Coordinate major group functions and be sure all team members are in synch.

Be available. While working with a group, assume a physical position among the team where you can view the group's work and offer influence as needed. Be close at hand but not on top of everyone. Move around as needed. Allow your team members to ask questions, but don't hover.

As the leader, you're accountable for the group's results. Encourage them; remind them of your goal. If appropriate, use a checklist—aircraft pilots always do. Praise the total group's effort, especially those responsible for extraordinarily good work. Correct errors afterward, aside from the group.

Overall, you're verifying that the job is done correctly, on time, at the right place, in the right manner. And you're making sure your group learned from the experience.

Get motivated

The great majority of people are motivated every day by external rewards. The most common example is employment: for a certain hours of work, a person expects to receive money in exchange. In school, a student might be motivated to earn good grades by his parents who allow her to obtain a driver's license when she reaches a certain grade point average. Other examples of rewards include extra time playing video games, access to the family car, movie tickets, or other tangible rewards.

Psychologist Andrew Maslow was the first to describe how people are motivated by different forces depending on their needs. Individuals without enough food to eat would likely be genuinely motivated if food was offered as a reward. The problem with external motivation is that they're usually based on transient lower level needs, so they only work for a limited period of time. As soon as you receive the reward, your motivation goes away too.

Create excitement

To build an effective team, find out what excites your team members, what motivates them, and over time, what inspires them.

Certain people are motivated by less tangible rewards. An architect might work extra hard on a project for the satisfaction of seeing his building constructed. In school, a number of students are motivated to earn good grades because they are interested in learning and improving their mastery. They like to learn because it's fulfilling.

When you're exerting control over a group, you're working to find out what motivates team members and help them to meet that need.

Build influence, develop respect

Influence is based on reciprocal respect, loyalty and trust. When you share information openly, give credit where credit is due, show humility, and demonstrate integrity, you gain influence and build respect.

When you communicate openly and honestly with your team members, you increase feelings of mutual trust and friendship.

Praise in public; criticize in private.

When you praise individual contributions in public, you build loyalty. When something doesn't happen as expected, offer criticism in private. Always give correction privately and without a judgmental attitude or tone. Don't point fingers, blame, or criticize.

Integrity and honesty are repeatedly cited as the number one attributes that people seek in a leader.

When people talk of the qualities they most admire, the most frequently noted characteristics are honesty, integrity, being a "straight shooter," saying what you think, and avoiding fudging the truth to please the group you're with.

Trust, loyalty, open communication and camaraderie are group characteristics that we typically associate with high-performing teams.

As a leader, you want to complete the job on time. You help make sure team members are appropriately dressed and equipped. You encourage everyone to do their best, see that work is properly delegated, and set a positive example at all times.

Reward success

Intrinsic control means to help team members find the internal motivation that propels them to success. To sustain control over a group, integrate what motivates individuals with the group's goals.

A team is most effective when the group members' intrinsic motivations are rewarded by the group's goal and direction. When you successfully sync individual motives and the group's vision, the group achieves awe-inspiring results.

Performing as a Team

When a group is working well together, they have figured out who they are and what they need to do. They know how to work together and have developed a sense of identity and loyalty. They are no longer merely a motely group of individuals, but have evolved in a team. They have joined together and are unified in pursuit of a common goal. Members are flexible and willing to help each other.

Team members are cooperating and collaborative. They feel loyalty to the team. The team has likely established an identity that is unique to the overall organization. As reflected in the origins of the word *team*, the group has come together like a team of draft horses to pull together.

The team and its goals are more important than any single member's individual goals. At this stage, your leadership role is more blurred—everyone is likely pitching in and getting the job done.

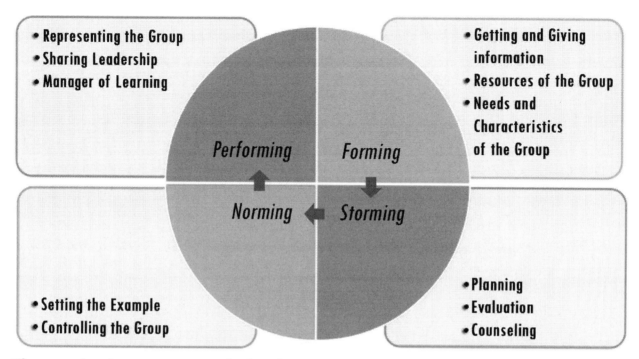

- **Representing the Group**
- **Sharing Leadership**
- **Manager of Learning**

- **Getting and Giving information**
- **Resources of the Group**
- **Needs and Characteristics of the Group**

Performing

Forming

Norming

Storming

- **Setting the Example**
- **Controlling the Group**

- **Planning**
- **Evaluation**
- **Counseling**

The group has become a team. Help them learn to represent the group, share leadership, and manage learning.

As a staff leader, depending on the age and maturity of your youth staff, you might not present these last three competencies to them. You have to assess their readiness and the needs and characteristics of individual members.

Use the last three skills to help the group hone its ability to get the job done and keep the group together.

These last three leadership skills are complex. They aren't usually presented to younger participants who aren't mature enough and who don't yet hold positions of responsibility where they are needed. As youth mature, they learn to be less self-centered and more sensitive to others. They gain compassion and greater insight into other people's behavior.

- **Representing the Group**. Clearly understand your team's goals, challenges, and opportunities and work effectively with other teams.

- **Sharing Leadership.** Select an appropriate style of leadership, from authoritarian to consensus. The style you choose is based on the situation and your leadership role.

- **Manager of Learning**. Help others learn is a skill that requires a large amount of experience and a comprehensive understanding. For instance, learn to understand the distinction between Manager of Learning as a leadership *competency* and Manager of Learning as a *concept* and *method* for leadership development.

Representing the Group

About Representing the Group

Representing the Group means to effectively interact with and accurately communicate your team members feelings, ideas, etc. to outside teams. It also means representing the other teams back to your team.

To represent your team effectively, you must know your fellow team members' needs and characteristics and understand your team's goals. As a representative, you're given the authority to speak for *and act* on behalf of your team or organization. Whatever decision you make, you're striving to both keep the team together and help it achieve its goals.

You must represent your team on a variety of issues. Sometimes you'll know about it in advance, other times you won't.

Other groups base their understanding of your group through you, the representative. You must be consistent, possess integrity, and be fair to all parties.

Representation is not democracy. In a pure democracy, every member of the team has an equal voice. In our modern, complex society, direct representation isn't possible. In our communities, as work and other projects grow in scope, team interactions rapidly become more complex. Our world has become a global community, and organizations are increasingly interdependent.

Information is passed from organization to organization, from team to team, at a blistering pace. Leaders at all levels must coordinate and communicate with a number of other organizations inside and outside their immediate team. Every group expects rapid turnaround of the decisions and information they need to conduct business.

Modern, effective leaders need to speak for their team, negotiate, receive and transmit information, be persuasive, and carry out many other responsibilities inherent in any leadership position. At one time, individuals specialized in a narrow profession and didn't need to know much outside the boundaries of their work.

Specialists as leaders. More and more companies today tend to push authority and responsibility closer and closer to the specialist, and every individual needs to be proficient in leadership skills. This includes the ability to cross team boundaries and represent their team. As young leaders acquire these skills, they're much better prepared to become successful business and community leaders.

To overcome these challenges, effective organizations have evolved methods of leadership that delegate responsibility and accountability to individuals who are actually completing tasks. In a political system, this is usually known as a *representative democracy*.

Objectives

When you complete presenting the content in this chapter, learners are able to:

- List four characteristics necessary to represent a group effectively.
- List four competencies that are important to representing the group.
- Name one reason representing the group important.
- List three ways to assess individual's feelings.
- List three action steps necessary while representing a group.
- List two steps to take after representing a group.
- Name one type of decision you probably should not delegate to the group.

Imagine

Since the service group approved the funding request for Kamping for Kids, they asked you to involve other youth from Regional Occupational Programs that specialize in law enforcement, hospitality, and emergency medicine to lead the event. They gave you names of four other teen groups and your team called all of them. Only three called back. You set up a meeting in two weeks.

Students from three high schools are planning to attend. One school specializes in culinary arts, or cooking. Another is a magnet school for students interested in law enforcement. The other has a program at the county hospital. They are from five to 40 miles away from your school.

Your group quickly agrees that they don't have enough people to do everything involved. They decide to brainstorm and develop a list of all of the tasks that have to be completed. Your advisor contributes a few ideas, and before long the list mushrooms to 58 items. But some of these ideas are complex and have many parts.

Your group decides to divide the list into tasks that need to be done right away and others that can wait. One of the most important pieces of information you need is how the other schools can help. You need to meet and coordinate what each of the schools will do.

In the last few minutes of the meeting, five people volunteer to contact the schools.

At your next meeting, the five representatives report back. One said they received an enthusiastic response from one school, who wanted a list of tasks they could do right away. She said she looked at her notes and gave them 15 items that your group hasn't done yet. When you look at the list of tasks she gave them, you see that your group needs to be in charge of three of them because they affect multiple schools.

Another representative says the schools he talked to are interested. The advisors wanted more information, but he said he didn't know where or exactly when the camp is being held, so he told them he'd call them back.

A third representative received a list from the schools of the number of students who attend the law enforcement programs.

The results from contacting the schools aren't helpful. A whole week has gone by and you're in the same position you were last week.

How are you going to persuade your group members to represent the group more effectively? What information where they missing that led them to produce such variable results? How are you going to fix the situation where one member gave away tasks that belong to your group? How much leeway does each representative from your group have when talking to the other groups?

You need to represent the group.

Get group input

Representing the Group is more an art than an exact science. When the requirement to represent a group regarding a specific issue is known beforehand, then the entire representation issue is much more manageable. It's an issue requiring decision making skill.

If you're effective at representing your group, you positively influence their attitude, motivation, and enthusiasm. They feel that what they think matters, that the ideas they develop are good, and that they're making a positive contribution to the entire group.

Get started

List four characteristics necessary to represent a group effectively.

There are four characteristics that help you faithfully represent your group to another group:

Get the facts. Make sure you fully understand the nature of the problem. Define who, what, when, why, where, and how.

Analyze the situation. If there's a problem, does the group need to give additional input, or can you make the decision? Determine the scope of the situation, the number of people involved, the amount of time available to make a decision, and the time available to implement your decision.

Validate the group's decision. Check to see if everyone in the group is in complete agreement. If there are differences of opinion, find out what they are. Be sure you fully understand how the decision (if any) was reached so to allow you to effectively communicate it to others.

Take notes. You can't accurately and responsibly recall the group's decisions if you don't' have an accurate record. Read your notes back to the group to confirm your notes are correct.

List four competencies that are important to representing the group.

Four competencies that are essential to effectively representing the group include:

Communication. First and foremost, make sure you're clearly communicating with your team members. It's essential to representing the group effectively.

Needs and characteristics. Assessing individual needs and identifying needs and characteristics helps the group find solutions while meeting everyone's needs.

Counseling. Use your reflective listening skills to make sure everyone's feelings and ideas are accurately heard.

Planning. Focusing on the task and help people overcome any inter-personal issues to help keep them moving forward towards their goal.

Name one reason representing the group is important.

Representing the group is important because it:

Keeps the group together. When team members believe their contributions are effectively represented, they feel more loyalty and satisfaction.

Helps get the job done. Our world is increasingly complex. It's extremely hard to do anything on your own. Reach out and connect with other groups and earn their support. When you effectively represent the group, you develop integrity and gain respect.

List three ways to assess individual's feelings.

Three ways to assess individual's feelings are:

Verify their commitment to their decision. If the group isn't locked into one option, you may be able to take several acceptable ideas to the group representatives for consideration. When group members are compliant, indifferent, or resistant to a decision, they may decide to ask you as their leader to represent them as uncommitted.

Take notes. As a representative, you're charged with carrying information not only to other teams, but from them back to your group. So you better be prepared. Represent the other team's point of view accurately. Whip out your trusty-dusty-ever-handy notebook and write a few key ideas down.

Ask questions. Once you've developed an assessment of the group's commitment to the decision, specifically ask them how much room you have to maneuver when it comes time to meet with the other groups. You may pose "if/then" scenarios to them: "If they want to do such-and-so, then would it be okay if..." and so forth.

Observe their body language. Watching someone's body language may reveal conflict between what they say and what they actually feel. You may notice someone is physically withdrawn from the group and isn't participating. That may be a clue that they don't fully endorse the group decision.

You may or may not want to tactfully help that person open up about what their feelings are. Depending on the circumstance, body language is difficult to observe, but it's a useful tool to help resolve differences before they surface later on.

Assess their commitment

When you meet with other group representatives, assess the other groups' commitment to their ideas. Make a decision all agree with. Weigh the other teams' commitment against your own group's commitment. Use a chart like that below to help you decide.

Situation	Your Group Is	Other Groups are	Your group is	Your action
1	Enthusiastically for	Decidedly against	Committed	?
2	Decidedly against	Indifferent	Committed	?
3	Indifferent	Enthusiastically for	Uncommitted	?
4	Enthusiastically for	Indifferent	Committed	?
5	Resistant	Indifferent	Uncommitted	?
6	Compliant	Decidedly against	Uncommitted	?

Your team is uncertain. If the group is neither decidedly against nor for a particular idea, then you as the representative might ask the group if you can represent them as uncommitted. This allows you to work with the other team representatives and find a suitable solution. (See situations 3, 5, and 6 above.)

Your team is committed. Every decision and situation is unique, containing situational factors that influence your decision making. If, for example, your group is wholeheartedly and unreservedly committed to their decision, but it's rejected by the other group representatives, return to your group and obtain more input. (See situations 1, 2, and 4 above.)

Once your team has made a decision, you as their leader are committed to it, even if you personally think and feel otherwise. Your time to voice your personal opinion is within the group. As their representative, you're now their voice. You don't speak for yourself.

Assuming the decision has been made to everyone's satisfaction, the representative simply bears the responsibility to represent his team thoughtfully and accurately. (He uses the Giving and Getting Information competency.)

List three action steps necessary while representing a group.

When representing the group:

Be accurate. State your team's position faithfully and accurately. If you disagree with selected parts of your team's decisions, you may be tempted to fudge when representing your group. Be faithful to their decision. The other teams won't accept 100% of everyone's input. It is extremely likely that there will be more time for additional ideas.

Listen carefully. Listen fully and respectfully to be sure you understand the other teams' ideas and points of view. If during the discussion someone provides new information that affects likely solutions, then a second round of decision making may be called for.

Identify and resolve conflicts. If there are conflicting opinions, decide how to achieve the goals of your group so that all are satisfied. You may need to renegotiate with the other group or teams.

Debrief afterward

List two steps to take after representing a group.

After representing the group:

- Carry the decision back to your group. Refer to your notes. You did take notes, didn't you?
- Explain the context for the decision to the group. Remember, you're now representing the group which made the decision back to your own group.

Wing it

No team input—now what? When advance notice isn't available, representation rises to an art form. Sometimes you're faced with the potentially difficult situation of representing your group without first having had a chance to obtain their input. You've built up trust and respect with your team.

But if the decision you are making is complex, you might be putting yourself in hot water, so proceed carefully.

If you only have to decide what the menu is for the next meal, that's one thing. But if you're asked to make a decision affecting how others, for example, spend their money—be careful!

Consider these questions before proceeding:

- What precedents within the group do you have to go on?

- How much trust does the group have in you?

- Has the group empowered you to act on your own and use your best judgment?

- How committed is the group to the issue and to their decision? How does this issue/decision rank from a larger perspective?

- What are the short- and long-term effects of this decision, and who does it affect?

- How well do you know your group members' needs and characteristics? Can you anticipate their concerns, objections, etc.?

- Can the group defer a decision until you are able to connect with your group? If the decision is especially important, you should insist on it.

Delegate it

Name one type of decision you probably should not delegate to a team member or the team.

As the leader, you're responsible for and accountable to your team.

Don't delegate important, long-term decisions. If a decision is likely to have a big impact, it's not wise to delegate. If you're faced with a critical decision that might have long-lasting implications or affects the entire team, you probably shouldn't delegate it.

You're the leader because of your high level of interpersonal skills, your tact, fairness, sensitivity and knowledge of team members and the job.

Non-critical issues. On the other hand, it's a good idea to delegate non-critical issues to team members and let them carry the ball when representing the group. This is a good opportunity to give them the opportunity to practice and improve their competence in Representing the Group. This helps the entire group to prosper.

Sharing Leadership

About Sharing Leadership

Sharing leadership means to vary your style of leadership depending on the team and the situation. Leadership styles generally range from authoritative to participative. Your goal is to grow your group until as a team they are able, ready, and willing to assume most of the responsibility for leading themselves.

When they're ready, they distribute the leader's functions among themselves. Shared problem-solving and decision making is an increasingly favored model of leadership world-wide because it's more cost-effective and efficient.

A few old style organizations foster styles of leadership that force individuals to compete for control of information and resources. They base the competitive idea on the theory that the strongest leaders rise to the top. But these types of practices are less and less responsive to our complex society today. Organizations with a single strong leader may actually be vulnerable and weak, because when they lose their primary leader, the remaining members are unready and unable to cope with issues and challenges.

Participation is key. Participative or cooperative styles of leadership are the key to our society's future. They foster a philosophy of distributing responsibility, control, and accountability to the lowest levels in the organization practical. Individuals at this level have the information and resources necessary to make immediate decisions critical to the organization.

When the Toyota automobile company allowed factory line workers to stop the assembly line when they spotted a defect, the number of defects dropped dramatically while the number of vehicles produced actually rose. The company realized significant cost savings because it was able to reduce the number of vehicles needing repair before they could leave the plant. Employee morale rose along with the quality of the work. There were fewer labor complaints and less downtime.

Objectives

When you complete presenting the content in this chapter, learners are able to:

- List five styles of leadership.
- List one situation where the telling style of leadership is appropriate.
- List two characteristics of the telling style of leadership.
- List one situation where the selling style of leadership is appropriate.
- List two characteristics of the selling style of leadership.
- List one situation where the delegating style of leadership is appropriate.
- List two characteristics of the delegating style of leadership.
- List one situation where the joining style of leadership is appropriate.
- List two characteristics of the joining style of leadership.
- List six forces acting on the leader and on the team that influence the appropriate styles of leadership.
- List four team maturity levels.
- List two situations when telling must be used.
- Name three reasons a leader would want to persuade the team
- List four situations when a leader should consult with the team
- List six reasons why a leader would delegate tasks to their team
- Name six guidelines a team should follow when joining
- List the style of leadership appropriate each maturity levels.
- State who is always responsible for the team.

Imagine

Your Kamp for Kids idea has taken on a life of its own. Thirty-two kids 11-13 years old are signed up. You've got a campground reserved, but there's a long list of things to get ready. You still need to organize transportation, pick up the donated camping gear, finish the menu, and order food. One adult has volunteered to serve as camp medic and another as cook. You have 18 youth on your team who are going to be at camp for late June.

You've come up with some goals for the week, including taking a hike. You need to find a trail for an overnight hike. Your team decides to scout out a possible hike in person next weekend, even though there's a slight chance of rain.

While on the hike, a member of your teams twists his ankle badly about a half-mile up a short, steep hill from camp. He's in great pain, and the one member of your team with first aid training thinks his ankle is broken.

Some team members think it's important to finish checking out the hike. The guy with the bad ankle tells the team to go ahead, he'll wait there by himself.

Your team needs to survey the route of the hike. The always enthusiastic volleyball team captain encourages everyone to keep going. Everyone brought rain gear, but the team is divided. Some want to take the hurt team member back into town right away. There's no cell service, so you have to decide on your own.

It's a little after noon. The clouds are getting darker and the wind is starting to increase.

What are your options? How do you decide who to follow? Who has the best and most accurate information about your situation? Which person do you trust the most? Whose feelings do you take into consideration first? Who decides?

Find your leadership style

List five styles of leadership.

Sharing leadership is a series of five leadership styles, from most to least authoritarian: Telling, Selling, Consulting, Delegating, and Joining.

Use these leadership styles in all types of situations in your school, community, and at home. Depending on the team you're working with and the job, choose a leadership style that fits the situation.

The leadership style you choose is based in part on the readiness and maturity of your team. The more ready and mature they are, the easier it is for you as a leader to choose a hands-off leadership style.

Telling

High job, low team. In the Telling style of leadership, you're usually more focused on the job and less on the team.

You assess the problem, consider alternatives, choose one, and take charge. You tell team members what to do. You may or may not consider how the team feels about your decision. In practice, you want to ask team members for their help, not tell or order them. Nobody likes to be told what to do unnecessarily.

Poor leaders sometimes turn telling into YELLING or negative variations like manipulation and coercion.

List one situation where the telling style of leadership is appropriate.

Emergencies. The team is usually not ready or able to act on its own. The telling style of leadership is suitable for situations requiring urgent action, like providing first aid to an injured person.

Simple situations. You might also use the telling style for simple situations that don't require much   thought or group input. For example, when a new person joins your team, tell (or ask) another team member to explain how the team operates, when it meets, team rules and procedures, and so forth.

Task-oriented work. The telling style of leadership is suitable for work environments like manufacturing where there may be a diverse group of people with a wide range of experience and maturity levels.

List two characteristics of the telling style of leadership.

The telling style shown below is characterized by:

- One-way communication.
- Authoritarian style of leadership.

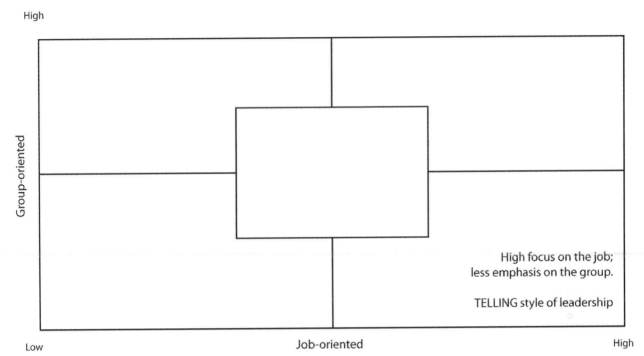

High

Group-oriented

Low   Job-oriented   High

High focus on the job;
less emphasis on the group.

TELLING style of leadership

Telling style of leadership.

Selling

High team, high job. You're using the selling style of leadership and are focused on both the job and the team. You may state the problem and decide what to do, selling others on your idea to gain support. You might explain how the idea benefits the team and attempt to persuade them to go along with it.

You still provide structure and make decisions. The major difference between the telling and selling style is that in the second style, you're persuading follower to understand and commit to the job at hand.

List one situation where the selling style of leadership is appropriate.

Getting buy in. For example, you may have what you think is a good idea for a community service project. When you describe the benefits of the service project to your team, they want to know, "What's in it for me?" You challenge is to first assess the needs and characteristics of your team. Then engage them in your cause and sell them on your idea.

List two characteristics of the selling style of leadership.

Selling is characterized by:

- Two-way communication.

- Support

- Positive reinforcement

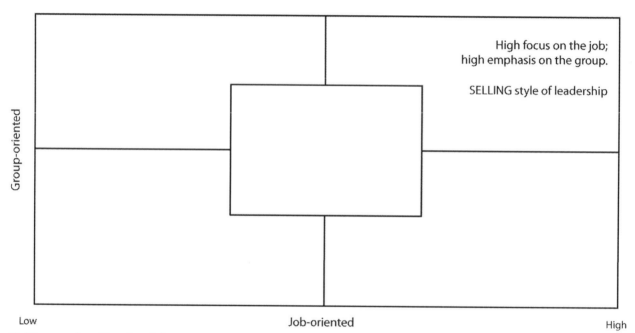

Selling style of leadership.

Delegating

Low team, low job. While you can delegate responsibility for a task, you can't delegate your accountability. Consider delegating non-vital tasks to team members that help grow their capacity and ability. Choose this style of leadership when the team is relatively mature and don't need your direct guidance.

List one situation where the delegating style of leadership is appropriate.

Motivate your team. As your team matures and becomes able to work more independently, reward and motivate them by delegating important tasks to them. When you show respect for people they are happier and feel more loyalty to the organization.

When risks are minimal. If the task is simple or relatively unimportant, delegating is a good choice. This gives team members the chance to run their own show. If something goes wrong, the consequences are minimal.

List two characteristics of the delegating style of leadership.

Delegating is characterized by:

Sharing information liberally. You fully describe the task to the team and give them all the information they may need to make effective decisions and take action.

Leading from a distance. You ought to step away from the immediate vicinity of the team. You have entrusted them with both the decision making and the outcome. If appropriate, observe and evaluate.

Even when you delegate, you retain responsibility, authority, and accountability. Both you and the team share the positive and any negative consequences.

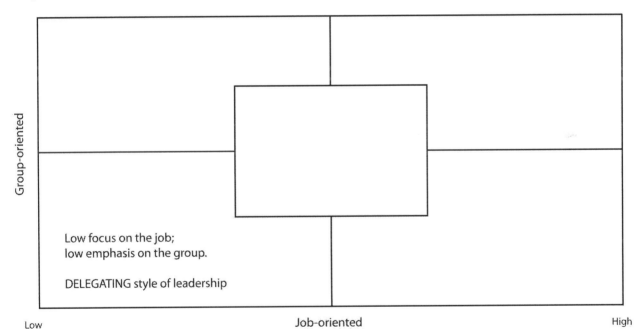

Delegating style of leadership.

Joining

High team, low job. When you join with the team to make decisions based on group consensus, you need more time. The leader isn't focused on either the team or the job—the leader is *part* of the team. The *team* is responsible for the group and the job.

This method works best when authority, responsibility, and accountability can be legitimately transferred to the entire team.

Even if the leader and the team don't choose to attempt to reach a consensus, the effective leader encourages active, equal participation, the expression of minority opinions, and acceptance of different points of view.

List one situation where the joining style of leadership is appropriate.

Shared accountability. To be effective, consensus requires total member participation, quite a bit of   motivation, and power distributed equally among all members. This method is frustrating to a "designated" leader who wants to reserve his right to authority.

Long-term impact. Consensus is especially suitable when you want to resolve complex problems that have a long-term impact on the team and require complete team support. However, reaching a true consensus—complete unanimity—can take more time than a few members may be willing to give.

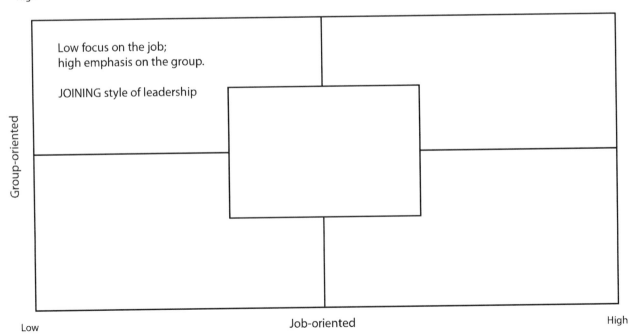

Joining style of leadership

List two characteristics of the joining style of leadership.

Key characteristics of decision making using joining or consensus are:

- Avoid arguing for your own individual judgments.

- Approach the task on the basis of logic.

- Avoid changing your mind only in order to reach agreement and avoid conflict.

- Support only solutions with which you're able to agree at least somewhat.

- Avoid "conflict-reducing" techniques such as majority vote, averaging, or trading to reach decision.

- View differences of opinion as helpful rather than as a hindrance in decision making.

Consulting

Medium group, medium job. In the consulting style of leadership, the leader states the problem and after consulting with team members, makes the decision for the team. The team members give ideas or input but the leader decides what to do.

List one situation where the consulting style of leadership is appropriate.

When you use the consulting style of leadership, you are equally focused on the team and on the job. You've built up a little trust with your team, and they give you input while allowing you to make the decision.

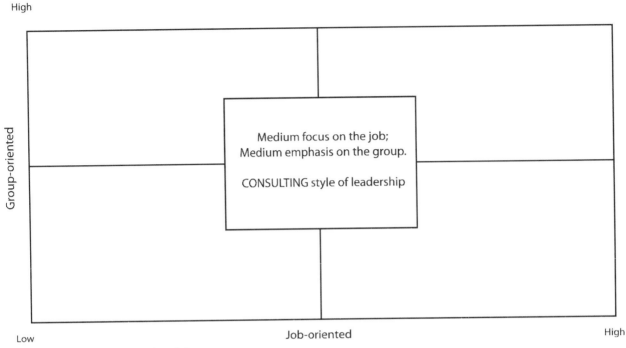

Consulting style of leadership

List two characteristics of the consulting style of leadership.

The consulting style of leadership is characterized by:

- Ongoing support to members.

- Two-way communication.

- Seek members' input into decision making.

- Focus more on the team and less on how the job.

- Members are primarily responsibility for getting the job done.

Balancing team and job. These styles of leadership are appropriate depending on the task, the situation, and the team. The talented leader uses the most appropriate style.

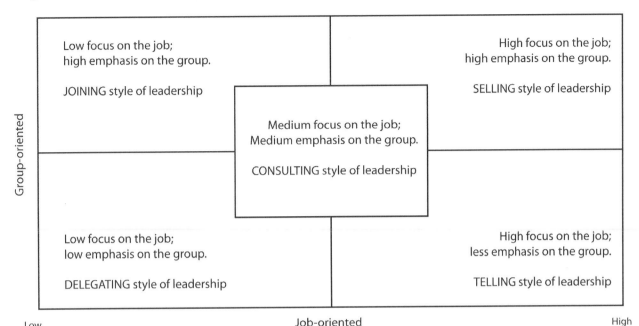

Sharing leadership – balancing keeping the team together and getting the job done

Forces affecting the leader

There are several forces affecting the type of leadership style available to the leader.

Influences on the leader

A number of forces or constraints affect which leadership styles are appropriate in any given moment.

Forces on leader. These include your knowledge, skills, attitude, experience, background, values, personal goals, team goals, confidence in members, convictions about styles and your choice of style, pressures from outside teams, time, resources, personality, sensitivity, weight of responsibility.

Forces on team. These include the combination of personalities in the team, values, expectations, willingness and ability to make decisions, individual needs, team needs, interest, competition, confidence, resources, work load, spirit, communication, and fatigue.

Forces on situation. These include time, organizational restraints, environment, scope or duration of job, conflicting goals, emergencies, hazards, desirability of the job, justice, ethics, legality, removal or lack of alternatives.

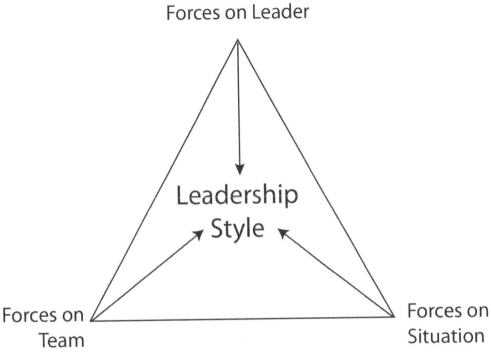

Forces affecting choice of leadership style

Influences on the team

The five styles of leadership previously described are useful ways to look at leadership, and they also happen to correspond to the Situational Leadership® model. It states that the leader determines the appropriate leadership style by identifying:

Objectives. What do you want to accomplish? (What are the team's objectives?)

Resources. Who are our resources? (What are the capacities of these resources? What relevant skills, knowledge, and abilities are present? What is the willingness and ability of those present to apply those talents?)

Individual maturity. How mature are the individuals and the team in its ability to both get the job done and keep the team together?

Forces affecting goals

A wise leader selects a style of leadership that not only fits the situation, but helps the team achieve its short- and long-term objectives. Consider how the current activity affects the teams' short- or long range goals.

Short-range goals

Short-range goals and objectives include temporary events and activities, like completing a certain task or learning a new skill.

Urgent action. Extremely urgent actions, like responding to emergencies, demand a telling style of leadership. "Let's help this guy push his car out of the sand!" These urgent actions obviously don't require writing objectives or huddling while you gather a team consensus. The leader leaps in and takes action without deliberating.

Important tasks. When time is short, use the Telling style to get the group moving.

Long-range goals

The forces affecting completing long-range goals are more difficult to manage. It's harder to think of ways to attain them. With long-range goals, it's a bigger challenge to sustain team members' interest.

Break 'em down. To make progress on long-range goals, the trick is to break the down into intermediate steps, or objectives, that are accomplished one step at a time.

The more long-range the goal, the more the leader needs everyone's participation in team decisions affecting the goal and their commitment to the result.

Recognize and reward participation. One way to encourage participation is to create special activities that reward participation. Events could include a high adventure trip like a river rafting trip. Reward high-achievers by giving them a chance to help others to learn what they know.

Good leaders recognize that the style of leadership they use affects how team and individual objectives are completed. An effective leader considers how to build the team over time, not getting the immediate job done. A few of these considerations are listed below

Goal	Description
Improve motivation of members	Lift their spirit, increase their morale. When members of a team share in making decisions, they're more willing to see the job through.
Improve quality of decisions	Two heads may be better than one—eight may be terrific. Pooling experience and judgment at the start may cut errors and time in the end.
Develop teamwork and morale	Morale is a symptom—so look for it. Making challenging decisions together helps build members into a real team. Give the team hard tasks and watch them grow.
Develop individual members	We all have our hang-ups. If something is hard for an individual, practice it within the team first. This can help members learn to do it individually. Decision makers are made by making decisions.
Increase readiness for change	Readiness to react to change and to anticipate and make changes. You learn by understanding and accepting responsibility for the consequences of your actions. When you make decisions as a team and live with them—that's living!

Factors affecting leadership styles

Factors affecting your leadership style. As a leader, you are usually focused on both short- and long-range goals. You choose a leadership style based on several factors:

- **Team and task related.** A few of your team and task goals have higher priority than others. The leadership style you choose reflects those priorities.

- **Individual readiness.** Your team members are at varying levels of readiness, ability, and emotional maturity. If your team and task focus doesn't fit the team's needs, choose an alternate leadership style that does.

For example, if your current emphasis is on improving the team, you might choose the Joining style of leadership. But if the team is unwilling and unable, choose an alternate leadership style, Telling, that matches the team's needs.

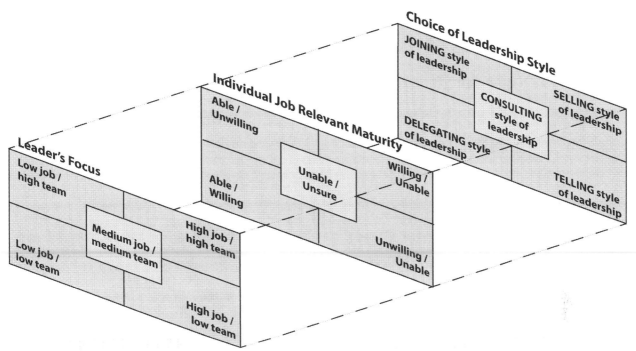

Select a leadership style based on your overall assessment of the team and of each team members' readiness and maturity. If they aren't aligned, choose an alternate style.

Neither willing nor able. The individual doesn't have the knowledge, skills, or ability to perform the job and is unwilling to try it without overt leadership (i.e., hand-holding). This can occur any time an individual confronts an unfamiliar job. For example, if you were to ask a team of brand new participants to design and lash a bridge together, they'd probably fall in the category of unwilling and unable.

This maturity level requires focus by the leader on the job at hand. Developing the team relationship is secondary. This is a high job/low relationship function. The Telling style of leadership is most appropriate.

Willing but unable. The individual doesn't have the knowledge, skills, or ability required but is willing to learn with the assistance of a leader. The individual needs ongoing leadership while they learn the job.

This maturity level requires the leader to focus on both developing the relationship and building up the individual's ability to independently perform the job. This is a high job/high relationship form of leadership. The Selling style of leadership is most appropriate here.

Unable and unsure. The individual isn't sure if he has the necessary skill or is unsure or hesitant to accept the responsibility given him. The individual needs coaching and encouragement to help him find out if he can do the job.

The leader is focused on both helping the team to work more effectively together and on getting the task completed. Depending on the team's progress, the leader consults with the team. He asks questions and is available as a resource. He helps team members find the knowledge, skills, and attitudes within the team to be successful. He takes the initiative when team members are unable to. This is a medium job/ medium relationship form of leadership. The Consulting style of leadership works best here.

Able but unwilling. An individual whose ability exceeds their willingness to work has an emotional block towards the job at hand. This is related to the individual's inability to imagine performing the job, or it may be based on an individual's hidden motives, perhaps due to a past failure in this area, or related to the individual's perception of unfair treatment by the leader or other members of the team. Thus they set out to minimize the success of the team and may even attempt to sabotage the team's ability to get the job done.

You must be sensitive to participants' needs. "First aid" counseling may be in order. You may spend time supporting individuals emotionally. You give more attention to the individual's needs than to the job at hand. This is a low job/high relationship form of leadership. The Joining style of leadership is best employed here.

Both willing and able. The individual wants to get the job done and has the ability to perform the job. The individual can work independently of the leader. This is a low job/low team form of leadership. A good leader would use the Delegating style of leadership is these situations.

Maturity levels

When approaching a given job, individual members of a team typically fall along a spectrum of maturity and emotional readiness levels:

- Neither willing nor able.

- Willing but unable.

- Unable and unsure.

- Able but unwilling.

- Both willing and able.

Member's readiness

Occasionally, you may find that for reasons you don't understand, team members are resistant to more participative styles of leadership. This resistance may be due to hidden barriers to effective team work, like these:

- Differing values
- Role conflicts
- Unclear objectives
- Dynamic environment
- Competition for leadership
- Lack of team structure
- Team membership selection
- Credibility of leader
- Lack of commitment
- Communication problems
- Lack of top-down support

Individual barriers

It may take careful questions from you to identify the problems keeping members from fully participating.

Two respected researchers in leadership, Hersey and Blanchard, have written extensively on leadership. They found that the single-most important factor a leader can use when selecting an appropriate style of leadership is an assessment of what they called the individual's "task-relevant maturity."

Hersey and Blanchard describe task-relevant maturity as the individual's capacity to get the job done in a high-quality manner, with a minimum amount of direction or control, while contributing to keeping the team together.

Leaders who work to get the job done and keep the team together are dependent on two factors:

Job maturity. The individual and team's ability to get the job done. This includes the knowledge and skills required.

Psychological maturity. The individual members' self-confidence, self-esteem, and maturity.

In other words, the team's task-relevant maturity is governed by their:

Their attitude. Their willingness to work independently, their motivation and orientation towards achievement.

Their skills. Their ability in the given technical area.

Their knowledge. Their experience in the relevant area.

Your youth leadership development program focuses on helping individuals develop the attitudes, improve the skills, and gain the knowledge required to become a leader.

Willingness

Willingness to grow. Characteristics of an individual who's willing to grow in their leadership capacity include:

- Self-starter
- Confident
- Hard worker
- Ambitious
- Energetic

Very few people naturally possess all these attributes. Most of us have to work to acquire these attitudes. So recognize that as leaders you must work with people at all levels to help them attain their goals.

Unwillingness to work. As a leader, you may run into individuals who aren't willing to do the work. They might show their reluctance indirectly, in a variety of ways:

- They insist the job isn't important.
- They procrastinate and avoid challenges.
- They start trouble and distract others from the job.
- They refuse to participate in the team or contribute to team-related tasks.

All of these and other behaviors are symptoms of an individual's lack of confidence in his ability to perform the job, or a lack of understanding about the importance of the job. They indicate that the individual may feel insecure, lack confidence—or more seriously—resist authority.

When evaluating an individual's ability to perform a job, remember that this evaluation is only relevant to the job at hand. It's unwise and inappropriate to generalize your evaluation of the individual to the rest of his life.

Readiness

Neither willing nor able. When an individual is neither willing nor able, your first responsibility is to help him acquire the skills required. New groups are usually in this phase.

Your job as a leader is to help them grow and change. As the learner achieves a level of consistent success, he desires more autonomy. You slowly cut back on structure and increase the emotional support you give to individuals.

You might give the learner small, bite-size pieces of responsibility that he can complete on his own. As the individual progresses, you recognize the individual's growth and reward him with public and private praise. Your team member recognizes, as they act more independently, that they are earning your respect, confidence, and trust.

Relationship strength

Another way of determining an appropriate leadership style is to assess the strength of team members' relationship with the leader, as shown below.

Relationship Strength	Best Style	Second "Best" Style	Third "Best" Style	Least Effective Style
Low	Telling	Selling	Consulting	Delegating
Low to Moderate	Selling	Telling or Consulting	Consulting	Delegating
Moderate to High	Consulting	Selling or Delegating	Selling	Telling
High	Delegating	Consulting	Selling	Telling

But in any situation, you must consider the appropriateness of each style relative to the forces generated by the situation and from within the team. Emergency situations don't lend themselves to consultation or delegation. You—the responsible individual with the attitude, skills, and knowledge required—need to take charge, now.

Sharing Leadership Method	Advantages	Disadvantages
Telling	Works well in crisis situations, when authority is without question.	Members may be uncooperative or resentful; they may not be prepared to respond to authoritative directions in a crisis.
Selling	Good idea when manager is most knowledgeable.	Members may not have sure commitment to idea.
Consulting	Takes advantage of knowledge that may be in team. Gets team members more involved, but let's manager retain authority, accountability.	Not all members may receive input or feel committed.
Delegating	Works well when manager has freedom to pass on responsibility and in situations when risk or consequences are low. Good way to give inexperienced members chance to practice.	Manager loses option to give input; decision may not meet needs of situation. If something goes wrong, manager has little chance to correct.
Joining (Consensus)	Best for decisions having long-term impact on whole team. High-quality decisions likely. Total team commitment needed	Takes more time. Requires informed team commitment to process. Leader must be able to give complete responsibility for decision to whole team.

Team needs

Match your style to the team. Suppose your team is well prepared and has made a decision about how to complete a certain task. But you stop them and attempt to persuade them about the merits of your plan. You're going to frustrate and de-motivate them in a big hurry.

Match your leadership style to the team and individual needs. The style of leadership you choose is a reflection on how effective you are as a leader.

Choose a leadership style to match the situation. The five styles of leadership are suitable to different situations. They're all valid ways to lead the team but a few are better than others depending on a variety of circumstances. Sometimes you have no choice but to tell the team what must be done. At other times, there are decisions so vital, everyone's input is essential.

Pass the credit, take the blame. Whatever style of leadership you use, as the leader you're accountable for the results. Excellent leaders strive to pass on credit for any success to the team, but protect the team when results go wrong by shouldering the blame.

There are two kinds of people, those who do the work and those who take the credit.
Try to be in the first group; there is less competition there. —Indira Gandhi

It's your job to be responsible—it's one reason why you are the leader.

Manager of Learning

About Manager of Learning

The phrase "Manager of Learning" isn't a new-fangled way to say "teacher"—it's describes a systematic method for helping people learn.

The emphasis is on learning, not teaching. Managing learning is a lot more than teaching. Knowing a skill doesn't mean you automatically know how to pass it on to others with ease. An experienced manager of learning is relying on skill and experience. They use these abilities behind-the-scenes to manage the team and weld them into a team.

Because learning is an ongoing, life-long process, managing learning is a cyclical, iterative process.

The discovery approach confronts the learner with a problem and requires their active participation to solve the problem. It goes way beyond memorizing information. It gives the learner an opportunity to understand relationships and reflect on those relationships. It helps the learner develop greater insights.

Background. Manager of learning was conceived by Dr. Béla Bánáthy. He noted Professor of Developmental Psychology Marianne Hedegaard's juxtaposition of two educational systems:

In the first, the learner reacts to the teacher's active role. The teacher selects content and experience and the learner reacts to what is presented. The teacher organizes the content and experience and the learner passively connects them. In addition, a learner's unique motives are rarely accepted or encouraged.

In the second system, the learner is in charge. The learner actively selects content and learning experiences and the learner actively organizes them. This book favors the second system.

Grow leaders, not followers. As a Manager of Learning, you have a wonderfully special and important mission: helping leaders have a lasting, beneficial effect on the lives of their fellow team members, and on the lives of others. Your goal isn't to find followers; your goal is to create more leaders. You have a special opportunity to facilitate learning through the Manager of Learning methodology.

Applicable anywhere. Use the Manager of Learning method in any learning situation. As you develop a deeper understanding of Manager of Learning, use this methodology to plan a series of leadership development activities that engage participants.

Objectives

When you complete presenting the content in this chapter, learners are able to:

- List the six steps of Manager of Learning.

- Identify who is the focus of a Manager of Learning session.

- Identify the primary difference between a teacher and a Manager of Learning.

- Identify which human sense is most effective in helping learners retain information.

- List two reasons Manager of Learning is an essential element of every learning experience.

- List three characteristics of Manager of Learning that involve the learner.

- List two reasons Manager of Learning is effective as a learning method.

- List two characteristics of an aha moment.

- List two ways to help learners open up to new answers.

- List two ways to help learners open up to new answers.

- List two purposes of a guided discovery.

- List three choices available to you when you complete a guided discovery.

- List three reasons to write objectives.

- List five characteristics of effective objectives.

- List five criteria of a SMART objective.

- List two reasons to use questions during a teach / learn.

- List three advantages of open-ended questions.

- List three characteristics of open-ended questions.

- List two ways to respond to unanswered questions.

- List three characteristics of an effective Manager of Learning.

- List four principles of an effective application phase.

- List two ways the learner can take home what they've learned.

- List two characteristics of servant-leaders.

- List four characteristics of high-performance teams.

Imagine

Congratulations, your Kamp for Kids is a reality. You got the funding. All the youth from the different groups decide to work together to teach the kids camping, first aid, cooking, and personal safety skills.

Now you need to decide exactly what you're going to do during the week. You need a plan for each day of the five-day camp.

You decide to make a list of the things you want to teach the kids during camp. Your sponsor at the service group requests that you measure what the kids learn during camp. You're trying to figure out how to do this when one of your members tells about a technique he read for measuring success using criteria called SMART. After she explains the concept to everyone, you contact your service group sponsor and she agrees with this idea.

It takes some time, but you break up the list of things you want to teach between the different Regional Occupational Programs that specialize in law enforcement, hospitality, and emergency medicine. Each group researches a list of possible learning activities related to their goals. They select a list of learning activities and develop a list of SMART criteria for the learning activities.

You bring everyone together and complete a plan for the week. You schedule each learning activity, list the resources needed for each one, and the SMART criteria that you've created for each.

You're ready for camp. To make it really easy to check your progress, you create a checklist of the SMART criteria. Every group plans to use the checklist during the week so you can know exactly what learning activities were completed and the specific learning objectives are completed.

The Manager of Learning process

List the six steps of Manager of Learning.

Manager of Learning is a six-step method for effectively facilitating learning. After establishing your goals and objectives, use this Manager of Learning process to guide learners through a series of deliberately crafted experiences.

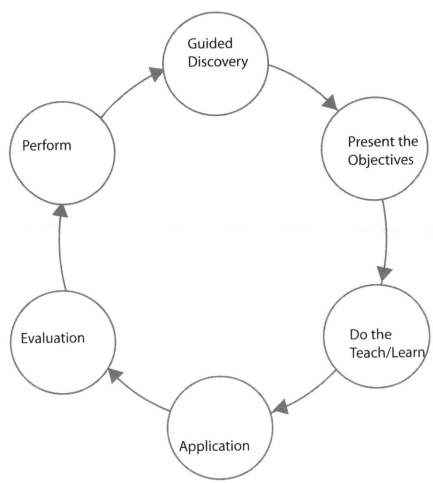

Manager of Learning is a six-step, cyclical, iterative process.

Focus on learning, not teaching

Identify who is the focus of a Manager of Learning session.

Your focus as a Manager of Learning during your learning session is on the learner.

A "Manager of Learning" isn't simply a teacher. Teaching connotes activities too typically requiring a lecture hall and a large number of desks. The phrase Manager of Learning is purposefully chosen. The emphasis is on *learning*, not on what the instructor *teaches*. Your job, as a Manager of Learning, is to help participants become more effective leaders.

Managers of Learning recognize that people learn as individuals, not as a class. They know each individual is important; therefore, each individual leader must learn or all receive an inferior program. Whoever accepts the responsibility for managing learning must use uncommon techniques to produce unusual results.

Teaching is about *learning*, not instruction. If learning is the true focus, then rigid scheduling like that in traditional classrooms is eliminated since individuals learn at different rates. Additionally, the learner is center-stage, rather than the teacher. The presenter is responsible for helping manage the learning environment.

Improve knowledge, skills and attitudes

When you *learn*, you gain *knowledge*, improve *skills*, and develop *attitudes*. Sometimes this is abbreviated to "KSA." Attitudes are obviously more important than skills or knowledge—after all, what is the barber going to do with that razor?—it might be better to turn it around and abbreviate it as ASK!

Identify the primary difference between a teacher and a Manager of Learning.

A*sking*, rather than telling, is the main difference between a teacher and a Manager of Learning. You ask, because maybe the learner already knows. Maybe they know but haven't realized that it applies in this situation. Or maybe they don't know they don't know. So ask him, first. Asking is the first of the four steps of Manager of Learning, the guided discovery.

Every successful leader requires a combination of attitudes, skills, and knowledge. Attitudes are the most important and the most difficult attribute of leadership to acquire. You must often replace an old attitude before you can adopt new skills or knowledge. The Manager of Learning must be able to detect this situation and know how to effect the change. Use counseling techniques to enable the learner to see a need for change—a change in attitude—and accept the help you or members of his team or others can give him.

The Manager of Learning recognizes that all learning doesn't take place in a fixed time or place—often understanding and capability bloom sometime after the seeds are planted.

As an unusually capable leader, the Manager of Learning is entitled to uncommon satisfaction. These is achieved from seeing a young leader progress through understanding towards proficiency. The Manager of Learning senses the urgency of the situation, yet has the patience to follow sound practices and avoid shortcuts that shortchange the learning experience. He struggles with each learner—knowing each person's needs to be different—and seeks the best way to reach him, not the "standard" way.

Evaluation is a "way of life" to the Manager of Learning. The Manager of Learning evaluates himself and his own methods, as well as those of the learner. This is a thinking person's role—not one for a programmed robot.

As a Manager of Learning, you experience ongoing growth. As you expect learners to grow, you are also growing. Each new experience gives you the chance to learn new knowledge, skills, and attitudes, and gain insights that enrich your life.

How people learn

To grow, you must change your behavior and how you think. You must move out of your comfort zone.

Life begins at the edge of your comfort zone. Be physically, emotionally, and mentally receptive to change. Start a hard task with an uncomfortable step.

Identify which human sense is most effective in helping learners retain information.

Learning requires engaging the senses. To communicate with a learner, you have to get his attention. Research has revealed that the more senses you engage to "paint" a new mental picture, the better the learner retains the information. When you activate his senses, you have the learner's attention and begin to erase mental roadblocks.

Touch. Of the five senses: hearing, sight, touch, taste, and smell, touch is most effective when used in combination with one or more of the other senses. That's because the person's entire being is engaged, blocking distractions, and helping the learner to focus on the new information.

For example, to help youth learn the importance of planning, the team was challenged to build a raft that could hold their entire group. The entire team had to pitch in and work hard to accomplish the task. During the activity, everyone was fully engaged. They had to use a variety of skills and share leadership.

If you're alert to meaningful learning activities that fully engage learner's body and mind, you become a tremendously effective Manager of Learning, and earn your team's respect.

A system for learning

Manager of Learning is a lot more than an instructional method. It's both a leadership skill you help participants learn and a key method you use to develop and present learning activities. It is the foundation to a philosophy of life-long learning.

List two reasons Manager of Learning is an essential element of every learning experience.

Manager of Learning provides a method for engaging the learner and challenges them to focus on only what they don't yet know.

A learning framework. Use Manager of Learning as the structure for all your learning experiences. Use the Manager of Learning method as a way to present all your learning activities.

Focused on the learner's needs. Each of the phases of the Manager of Learning process is dependent on the others. The Manager of Learning process isn't lock-step but at the learner's own pace of discovery.

Requires discovery activities. Begin the learning process with a hands-on *guided discovery*, a hands-on activity that reveals what participants know and don't know. If you always assume learners know something about what you are presenting—and they almost always do—you can use those individual's talents during your presentation and show respect for them.

Engages the learner. Manager of Learning works because it challenges and engages learners. It's different from classroom learning, where people are usually required to think linearly, to memorize facts, and to prepare for tests. But we know that's not how people prefer to think. Our minds like to find patterns and connections.

Use questions to draw the learner deep into the learning process. Questions help learners develop a feeling of self-discovery. Asking questions encourages ownership of the learning experience and helps individuals retain what they are learning.

Involve the learner

List three characteristics of Manager of Learning that involve the learner.

Manager of learning uses a *heuristic* approach that engages learners. Heuristic learning:

- Is open-ended.
- Stimulates imaginative thinking.
- Develops self-reliance and self-confidence.
- Focuses on problem-solving.
- Encourages self-discovery.
- Requires participation throughout.
- Not confined to one "right way."

- Is cyclical and iterative.

Why Manager of Learning works

List two reasons Manager of Learning is effective as a learning method.

Manager of Learning works because it:

Readies the brain for learning. By engaging learners in physical activities that require them to move, you're preparing them to learn—and remember.

Research has found that learners who are more active have greater attention spans, improved cognitive abilities, and increased blood flow. All of these help learners remember better. Practically, no one likes sitting all the time. A tired body helps the brain to focus.

Focuses on the practical. It stresses the practical aspects of the leadership job and presents information in a real-life context if possible.

Presents ideas in context. It presents concepts only when applicable to the task and presents them within the frame of reference of the specific task.

Motivates a desire to learn. It introduces a series of leadership tasks that increase the trainee's desire for knowledge of new principles, attitudes, concepts, skills and techniques.

Models real life. When feasible, present learning in the same sequence as it is needed during an actual leadership task.

Recognize "aha moments"

As a Manager of Learning you have an opportunity to guide and influence people during critical points of personal growth. When a learner suddenly gains a new insight, they are open to new ways of thinking.

Before you have an aha moment, you're typically stuck and can't figure something out. You've been thinking about the problem for a while.

List two characteristics of an aha moment.

Characteristics of an aha moment include:

Sudden inspiration. An aha moment is "a moment of sudden realization, inspiration, insight, recognition, or comprehension."

Ease. In a flash of insight, the solution suddenly appears and is immediately obvious as correct.

Positive moment. An aha moment is a positive physical, emotional, and mental experience.

Correctness. When achieving the insight, you immediately recognize its correctness even before you validate your reasoning.

Watch for learnable moments

Motivate learners to open up. Aha moments usually occurs when the learner is engaged but stuck. Your challenge as a Manager of Learning is to create situations that motivate the individual to actively participate and seek solutions to issues and problems.

Your goal is to help participants be open to new ways of thinking that prime the individual to accept a new idea or concept. These can become a memorable event for an individual.

Engage and challenge members. Your learning activities need to engage and challenge individuals with new learning situations. You want to arouse in them a need to alter their thinking and open them to new ideas. Your goal is to lead them to recognize that they're missing something and create a desire to learn more.

List two ways to help learners open up to new answers.

To help learners open up to new answers:

Listen to learners. When managing a learning experience, observe and listen to participants. They may say to each, "I don't get it." Pay attention to what learners are experiencing sometimes requires you to temporarily put aside your preconceived ideas and expectations about what they are learning. Pause and take in what's actually happening instead of looking for what you expect to happen.

Observe their body language. You may recognize that a learner is stuck and doesn't understand what you're presenting. They have a puzzled expression, are inattentive, fidgety, look reflective, or use other body language that indicates they are figuring something out.

From what they say. Learnable moments also occur during 1:1 counseling or conversations about personal subjects. You may notice that the learner you're talking to is stuck in a particular way of thinking. This is your chance to add information that might clarify their thinking.

As a Manager of Learning, you learn as much as the learners, usually more. When learners are interested and motivated, it's rewarding when you "see the lights go on" as people gain new insights.

Create learnable moments

Be responsive and alert to the situation and to opportunities that help you reach your goals.

List two ways to help create learnable moments.

Prepare the learning activity beforehand. Plan and prepare each learning activity with a purpose. Identify your goals and objectives. Require the learner to demonstrate a specific behavior. Make the learning activity challenging enough that it gets the learner thinking about your goals and objectives.

A few Managers of Learning are tempted to rely on unplanned events, unexpected problems, and chance issues encountered by the team as a source for learning.

Taking advantage of spur-of-the-moment challenges is rewarding and stimulating, but be careful. The ability to create a learnable moment on the fly requires considerable experience and sensitivity to the team's needs and characteristics.

Focus on your goals. These types of opportune moments takes skill and good judgment to be sure they reinforce and support your goals and objectives.

You're more likely to accomplish your goals by planning ahead and using pre-designed learning experiences. If you don't plan ahead, you're relying on luck, and the results are unlikely to be linked to your objectives. It might even lead your learners wildly off course, distract them, and require extra effort to re-focus the team.

Guided discovery

A pre-assessment. Once you complete your learning session, compare the learners' performance at the beginning to what they know at the end. This helps both you and the learners validate what they gained from the learning experience. It's like a pre-test, but without paper.

But it's much more than finding out what the learner already knows. You want to grab the learner's attention.

Involve the learners

An attention-getting activity. You want to create an attention-getting activity that requires the learner to apply knowledge, skills, or attitudes he may not yet have acquired. Use the guided discovery to prompt the learner to think about "What do I know about this?" or "How well can I do this?" or "What do I think about this?"

Learn what the learner knows

List two purposes of a guided discovery.

A guided discovery has two purposes:

The learner finds out what they don't know. The guided discovery helps the learner figure out what they know relative to your learning objectives. Now they're more motivated to pay attention and learn something they don't already know.

You discover what the learner already knows. The guided discovery helps you to assess learners' current knowledge relative to your learning objectives. Now focus on the specific information the learner needs. If you find any members already know a part of the subject, involve them in the learning activity. Give them a way to learn and grow by encouraging them to help less knowledgeable learners.

Your goal is to create within learners a need to know, to do, or to feel something specific. You want to find out how far they have to go to complete your learning objectives. This allows you to adjust your learning activities and content relative to what they already know.

Purposeful and pre-planned

Activate the learner's interest. Your guided discovery is most effective when you plan a purposeful, structured, hands-on experience that requires the learners' participation and generates interest. Focus their attention on the skill and what they know—and don't know.

Use the guided discovery to help the learner understand why they need to know the information you're presenting. Your goal is to make the discovery process fun and activate the learners' inquiring mind. These steps make the next teach / learn phase personal and meaningful.

If during an unrelated activity the learner accidentally learns they don't know something, this isn't a guided discovery.

Example: if the learners are cooking dinner, and someone forgets to tell the new cook they have to boil the potatoes before mashing them, this isn't a guided discovery for Giving and Getting Information. It's an opportunity to reinforce the importance of communication, but it's not a preplanned learning experience.

Calling any type of accidental learning a guided discovery blunts the effectiveness and usefulness of a designed experience.

Enhance knowledge, skills, and attitudes. One of the differences between the Manager of Learning method and standard teaching methods is that it aspires, through repeated experiences, to help learners enhance their knowledge, skills *and* attitudes. A single learning experience is inadequate; leadership skills are extremely difficult to understand. They're considerably more abstract than camping skills.

You know what they know

When the guided discovery is complete, both you and the learner have an informed understanding of the learner's current knowledge level. Now you know how to proceed and what to include in your learning activity.

List three choices available to you when you complete a guided discovery.

Now you have three options:

- **Start**. **Begin at the beginning**. The learner doesn't know anything. You might think that the learning activity was a flop or a failure. But the learning activity accomplished its purpose: it revealed what the learners don't know. That makes it a big success! Consider what needs improvement. Add new ideas that support your goals.

- **Stop**. The learner already knows what you want to help them learn. There's no point in going forward, Smile, congratulate them, and take a break. Later on, evaluate the team's needs and characteristics. Find out why your estimation of what they know was so inaccurate.

- **Continue**. **Subtract what they already know.** The learner knows a portion of your learning material, so start from there. You've need to be nimble and responsive when this happens. Make on-the-spot adjustments to your learning material. If a few learners know more than others, this is your chance to motivate the advanced learners by involving them in helping the less advanced.

Present the objectives

Before you begin, know where you're going. Based on your program's goals, define your learning objectives. While a number of people confuse the two, the words *goal* and *objective* serve completely different masters.

As steps are to a staircase, objectives are to goals.

As described in *Planning* on page 81, a goal is an "achievement that moves you closer to your vision." An objective on the other hand is *specific, measurable,* and *observable.*

Write worthwhile objectives

Anything that's worth learning is worth defining. If you can't define what you want to communicate, how do you know if the learning session is worthwhile? When you clearly state what you want learners to gain from the experience, they learn the value of the activity. They are more motivated because they understand why they are asked to complete certain tasks and activities.

Anything worth a moment of instruction is worth an hour of writing objectives.

List three reasons to write objectives.

Well-written objectives help you:

Identify the behaviors desired. This helps you select useful learning activities, and those let you figure out what materials, time, people, locations, and other resources required.

Give team members a reason to belong. Objectives ought to be specific so everyone on the team can buy in. Otherwise you're left with a profoundly subjective feeling of your success. "If you don't know where you're going, you won't know if you get there."

Communicate your intent. If you can't define objectives, then you probably haven't thought through what you want to do well enough.

Pin down your content. They describe the exact information you want to communicate to learners.

Tell the learners what they're learning. Writing objectives helps you document your progress towards your goals.

Inform parents, coaches, and leaders. Well-written objectives keep leaders and other interested individuals informed about what their youth are learning.

One of the biggest challenges for most programs is the "slip between the lip and the cup" when youth go home. To help youth put to work what they've learned, clearly explain what they are learning to the learners and others.

Allow you to evaluate your results. Objectives help you validate your program's effectiveness and plan on ways to improve. When you write down and evaluate your progress, you learn whether you're on the right track and what corrections you must make to continue progressing towards your goals.

A plan is made up of a number of linked objectives. When you define an objective, you're defining what success looks like.

Define your objectives clearly

To present learning effectively, clearly and plainly describe the desired outcomes of your learning experience. Once you've recorded that information, you're prepared to tell the learners what the learning experience is about.

If you don't know where you are going, you'll end up someplace else. — *Yogi Berra*

When you tell the learners the learning objectives, it's a good idea to print them on a wall chart, flip chart, or hand them out. This way everyone can easily refer to them.

List five characteristics of effective objectives.

An effectively written objective breaks down a goal into statements that meet specific criteria.

- An objective is precise and can only be interpreted one way.
- It's written from the point of view of the learner.
- It describes an observable behavior.
- It specifies the conditions under which the objective must be completed.
- It specifies the criteria for success.

A goal describes in general terms who and what is being accomplished. An objective is a standard or test used to measure the success of the learner. The criteria you use to define you objective must be observable, explicit, and measurable.

For example, if you wanted to have a competition to see which team can build a fire the fastest, you might write an objective like this:

Using the materials provided, build a campfire and burn through a string 24" above the fire in less than 1 minute.

Write SMART objectives

Objectives are difficult to write well, and it's important to take the necessary time! Well-written objectives enable you to literally check off your progress towards your goal.

As you write an objective, figure out how you're going to know whether the learner actually gets anything out of the learning experience. What a waste of your time if they don't!

When I was growing up I always wanted to be someone. Now I realize I should have been more specific. — *Lily Tomlin*

To write learning objectives that mean something, you need to be SMART.

List five criteria of a SMART objective.

Effective objectives meet the SMART criteria.

S	Specific	Is the item specific? Can it be accomplished? What is its impact?
M	Measurable	Is the item measurable? How can you know when it's done? Can the progress be tracked?
A	Appropriate	Is this task within your area of control? Does it need to be done? Is this an opportunity that is available to you?
R	Realistic	Can the item be accomplished? Can it be brought to a successful conclusion? Do you have control over the task?
T	Time-bound	Can it be done in a timely manner? Is it going to take too much time to accomplish? Can it be done in a reasonable time?

When you write objectives that meet the SMART criteria, you're letting participants know what's expected of them. They can quickly and easily figure out if they've actually learned anything. And when you evaluate later on, knowing what's been completed is a big plus.

Describe behavior

Objectives define visible behavior: an action, activity, or process that be observed and measured.

An objective is an observable behavior your grandmother can see.

An objective is so obvious that if you asked your grandmother to watch, she could see it happen. In other words, it must be specific and easily understood by individuals who aren't part of your team. It's plainly observable, not something you infer from or guess based on what the learner said or did.

Within the ability of the learner. The objective must be within the *ability* of the performer and *attainable* within the time allowed. It should be appropriate to the context and learning and not frivolous. The team must have access to the resources required to *accomplish* the objective.

Are realistic and attainable. The objective should be realistic given the available *time*, *personnel*, and other *resources*. There should be a high likelihood that participants can accomplish the objective. The participants must have the *control* necessary to complete the objectives.

Within a specified time limit. The learners are able to complete the objective within a reasonable and specific time limit, or must be accomplished by a specific point in time. If you can't apply a time limit to an objective, it's likely a goal, and you must break it down into more discrete segments that are measurable.

Reveal your objectives

Depending on your topic and learning methods, you may choose to reveal your objectives to the learners before or after the guided discovery.

Sometimes it's useful to keep your objectives private until the learners complete the guided discovery. If you reveal them beforehand, it can give the learners information that makes the guided discovery less valid or useful.

Don't read your objectives to the learners. They'll never remember what you said. Give each participant a printed copy of your objectives. Now they know what you want them to learn! They can also take the list of objectives with them. Alternatively, post a copy of the learning objectives on a flip chart where everyone sees them.

Teach / Learn

Once you've communicated your learning objectives, begin your teach / learn session. The learners have now figured out there's something worth learning—based on what they gained from the guided discovery—now it's your turn to kick into high gear. It's time to present information, to fill in the gaps, and help participants learn.

Know your audience

Before you prepare your learning experience, know your audience. Learn their needs and characteristics, experience, background, and readiness to learn. When you know your audience, you're able to relate new information to their past experience and knowledge.

The guided discovery opens their minds. Now begin to add information to what they already know.

Review the guided discovery. The guided discovery tells the learner and the leader what the participant knows about the subject. You need to put this information to use when you begin the teach / learn phase, otherwise your guided discovery is worthless. You've missed your chance to motivate the learner.

Consider your objectives. The teach / learn phase is your time to communicate your learning objectives. Depending on what you discovered during the guided discovery, adjust your content and select the information you want to include.

Avoid teaching. Throughout this book, we strive to avoid referring to learning activities as teaching or training. Your focus is on the learner. During all of your development and learning activities, remember to concentrate on participants and their experience. Your goal isn't to communicate a predetermined lesson, or to train a participant in a specific skill. Your goal is to help participants develop their capabilities as leaders.

We use the phrase "teach / learn" in this instance to describe the interactive give and take that is present during an effective learning session. Ideally, the process of "filling in the blanks" – the information learners don't yet have – is an active discussion that engages the learner.

Don't lecture

The lecture method was first used before the printing press was invented.

Lectures date from the 14th century. There was a time before we were born when books were rare and expensive. Copying books by hand took months. As a result, in that time and day, the lecture was conceived as the most effective way to communicate large amounts information to a number of people in the shortest amount of time.

Today, everyone hates lectures. They are the deadliest form of instruction in use. Unfortunately, that's all a few teachers know. They default to this method because of the size of the class they are required to teach, or due to the difficult dynamics of involving students who aren't always motivated. As a result, some teachers lecture. But because teachers use it doesn't mean it's a good model.   .

If you lecture, participants may die of boredom, and your organization's liability insurance probably doesn't cover it.

Avoid video and slides. Right up there with deadly lecture is the equally lethal video, first cousin to toxic digital slides.

Don't bore your learners with a video or your awesomely animated slides. After all, what do you do with your video or slick digital slides when 80% of the people already know 50% of your material? A few organizations require video and slides because they want to present the same material the same way all the time at every location. They assume of course that every learner is a blank slate, knowing nothing. As a learner, it's a terrible experience.

One exception is to present information that cannot be communicated by any other means, like a documentary. Another exception is to watch a film with the goal of stimulating analysis and discussion, like *Twelve O'Clock High*. But don't lecture. *Ever*.

Manage the learning experience

Review your learning objectives. As described earlier, you began by deciding what you want the learner to be able to do and how well you want them to perform.

During the actual learning experience:

- It's better to cover a few points well than many poorly.

- Be realistic. Only include objectives that you have time for.

- Over-prepare in case participants know more than you expect.

- Use instances from real life and stories: anchor what you say in concrete, relatable examples.

What you know isn't as important as what the learner knows and can gain from their own experience.

Choose learning methods

Choose learning methods that are flexible and adaptable to varying learning needs.

Match methods to the learners. Based on your objectives and what you know about the learners, select suitable learning techniques. There are lots of means and schemes that have been created over many years to communicate information between presenters and participants. You want to choose methods that stimulate participation, collaboration, interaction, and hands-on learning.

Watch for instant feedback. As you become more accustomed to making presentations before a group or audience, you begin to read the signs of acceptance—or the signals of danger—in your audience. If question marks appear on the foreheads of more than a few people, you're in trouble unless you sense what is wrong and take steps to correct it. Shifting positions in chairs, crossing and uncrossing of legs, yawning, droopy eyelids (or snoring) may tell you you've about had it.

Glances at watches (or worse, the calendar) may mean you have gone overtime. Throat clearing, drooping heads, people shifting in their chairs, and coughing may not be so much the symptoms of sickness as the symptoms of boredom. Hopefully, the more accustomed you become to working with groups, the better the signs are—questions, smiles, nods, note taking, brightened eyes, inching forward in the seats, exchanged glances—these are of the positive and encouraging symptoms of success.

Vary your learning methods. Use a wide variety of learning activities to communicate your content. Using any one method again and again, no matter how well it's handled, is boring and frustrating for both the learner and the Manager of Learning.

List resources required. When you choose a learning method or plan a demo, be sure to identify the resources required. If a role play is part of your plans, document the roles you need to explain to participants.

Rehearse. If you haven't used a learning method before, rehearse. Practice with any props and then make sure all your resources are on hand before beginning.

Be flexible. Use the learning methods in the following table during any phase of the Manager of Learning process.

Examples. Use buzz groups during a guided discovery to break the team into small groups who compete against each other. Use buzz groups during a different teach / learn session to encourage everyone involved to answer specific questions. Or use buzz groups during evaluation of another learning session to find out if everyone agrees about the progress made during the overall session.

Learning Method	What it is	How it works	When to use it
Seminar and Discussion	Talking to a team from previously prepared notes. Minimum seminar, maximum team participation. Discussion of a problem common to all. Conclusion reached by learned responding to guided questions.	Counselor or specialist presents information on a given subject. Counselor uses provocative questions or statements, usually prepared in advance, to stimulate team thinking and contributions to guide discussion.	When few if any members of the team are familiar with the subject and when a large amount of information must be presented. Team has knowledge or experience in the subject.
Small Team Discussion	Teams of 20 or less meet to address specific issues.	Run by a leader or facilitator. People are encouraged to speak openly and frankly. Results are reported back to the larger team.	To foster participation in workshops, seminars, roundtables, study circles, or Samoan circles.

Learning Method	What it is	How it works	When to use it
Panel Discussion	One or more specialist present short talks on a given subject, followed by questions and discussion.	Counselor/ moderator introduces specialist, later facilitates questions and answer period.	If the viewpoint of specialists serves a direct development need.
Quiz	Written or oral questions on performance of a job.	Trainer provides questions to individual or team.	To stimulate interest by pretesting. To determine knowledge of a subject. To identify what learners already know.
In-Basket	Learners respond to a situation based on what they might find in their "in-basket" on a typical work day, usually containing more than can be reasonably handled.	Learners use only their own resources in a limited amount of time to put everything in the "out-basket".	With single trainees when "paper" symptoms are significant.
Jigsaws	Participants put together pieces to make a completed "picture."	Individuals are each given parts of a design or organization and create a "whole," Examining all possible alternatives.	Useful in developing problem-solving, organization, or synthesizing skills.
Action-mazes	A "programmed" case study or branching tree.	Learners receive enough information to reach a decision point. The instructor provides the consequences of their decision and the next "frame."	To promote debate, dissent, confrontation, and compromise, with a specific objective in mind.

Learning Method	What it is	How it works	When to use it
Case-studies	Learners receive printed description of problem situation.	Selected detail adequate for a specified outcome (e.g., decision, recommendation) is proved with an identified outcome in mind.	To avert the tendency to avoid real issues by talking about theory rather than application.
Simulations	Extended role-plays with extensive design.	Teams of learners are given critical data about a situation, make their decisions, receive feedback, and take further action.	For team-building activities or for several teams at once.
Assigned Project	Counselor assigns one or more developmental task(s). Finding the solution to a given problem, checking a procedure with a qualified trainee/ specialist or written sources	Familiarizes learners with actual on-the-job, hands-on experience, individualizes development. Helps in solving a special problem.	Requires clear briefing, needs supervision. Not as effective with large teams.
Buzz Groups	A large group is split into several discussion groups followed by reports from appointed chairperson of each smaller group and summary by representative.	Individual expression, pooling of many ideas. Develops leadership skills. Mixes inexperience with experience. Permits joining of ideas. Allows opinions to be aired.	Can get side tracked. Domination by one or few. Questions must be provocative.
Exhibit	Actual objects, specimens, models, mock-up, graphic aids are placed on display with	Orientation, demonstration, attractiveness, home-made or professional. Publicity, bulletin boards readily	Extra time to prepare. Requires special place. Can be expensive. Requires special display skill. Distracting if in

Learning Method	What it is	How it works	When to use it
	appropriate captions.	available.	constant view.
Games	From the simple to the complex, a test of competitive and cooperative behavior in a light, sometimes humorous way. .	Prescribed rules limit behavior, encourage playfulness, to reveal sometime covert behaviors, or lead players to overt conclusions.	To emphasize general principles, to develop specific skills, to create greater involvement
Brainstorming	Everyone contributes as many ideas as possible. Quantity is the goal.	A facilitator or leader encourages input. Piggybacking on other ideas is encouraged. Avoid criticism of ideas. Record ideas for later evaluation.	To create innovative new ideas, encourage everyone's participation, draw out team expertise.
Role plays	Learners try out behaviors in a simulated situation in a limited amount of time.	Presenting conclusions isn't important, trying out behaviors is. Roles from life can be switched, all given a change to both play and observe.	To stimulate involvement, variety, reality, and specificity; to try out fearful behaviors, to check alternatives, with minimal risk.
Fish Bowls	Members sit in the center, while others observe, later to switch places. A vital topic is picked for team action.	After the fishbowl and its content, all discuss the experience to reach further conclusions about team process.	When there is greater concern with team process over course content.
Incident Process	Learners begin with inadequate data and ask questions to reveal additional information.	Presenter has all data, reveals limited amount to start, more in response to specific questions, for team to reach decisions.	To teach skills of interrogation, analysis, and synthesis relevant to problem solving and investigative techniques.

Engage the learners

Select learning methods that challenge participants, excite their interest, and are compatible with your topic. If possible, involve the learner with hands-on activities. Would you rather watch a video about making brownies or actually make them yourself—sneaking a little of the batter to make sure they taste good?

You're here to learn, and I'm here to present. If you stop learning before I stop presenting, please let me know. —Anonymous

Ask questions

To actively engage learners, ask questions! This is how you involve them and figure out in real-time whether or not they're actually learning anything.

Wait for answers. When you ask questions, don't join in the discussion with answers. That's not your role. If you do, participants may hesitate to answer further questions, or your answers may be accepted as "expert opinion" with no further discussion. If they ask you a question, boomerang it back to the team, if appropriate: "John's question is, 'How many days should our service project be?' What do the rest of you think?"

List two reasons to use questions during a teach / learn.

There are two main reasons to use questions during a learning discussion:

Discover what the learner knows. Help the learner to find out how much they know about the subject.

Provoke thought and evoke expression. Ask open-ended questions that stimulate the learner to think. Ask questions that provoke the learner to take a position or make a commitment and then challenge him (in a non-threatening manner!) to explain and defend his opinion. It takes a few seconds for people to engage their brains. Wait five to 10 seconds for an answer. That doesn't seem long, but stop right now and count slowly to ten. It feels like an eternity when you're standing in front of a group and nothing is happening. But educators have proven that when you wait, you receive better quality responses.

Vary your questions. Develop questions that are first broad and general. Then develop questions that are narrow, personal, and specific. Move back and forth like this during the Teach and Learn phase. Write down questions that help the learner to bridge from what they already know to what you want them to learn.

Learners reason best from the known to the unknown

Always think about the subject from the youth leader's point of view.

Use open-ended questions

One effective way to engage learners is to ask open-ended questions. It's a good idea to write questions before hand. Developing open-ended questions is one of your most challenging jobs as a Manager of Learning.

List three advantages of open-ended questions.

There are numerous advantages of open-ended questions.

Reflection. Open-ended questions encourage learners to think for themselves. You're helping learners to "connect the dots", to see relationships between ideas, to uncover links they hadn't considered. Unlike school, where the teacher is usually looking for one right answer, you are encouraging learners to make associations, discriminations, comparisons, and judgments.

Engage the learner. As you learn to ask open-ended questions on the fly, you're able to respond to the immediate needs of the learner and the dynamics of the learning activity. Always wait 5 seconds or longer for answers. More youth respond and you hear better answers.

Learners feel ownership. When you ask open-ended questions, you steer the discussion toward the learning objectives. As learners respond, they feel more ownership about the knowledge they're gaining.

List three characteristics of open-ended questions.

Characteristics of open-ended questions include:

Stimulate thought. An open-ended question stimulates a meaningful answer. It provokes thought, not an argument. Open-ended questions usually begin with "why," "how," or "Tell me about..." It is the opposite of a closed-ended question which only requires a "yes/no" answer.

For example, instead of asking "Did you learn anything from the guided discovery?" ask, "Tell me what you learned during the guided discovery."

Combines new information with old. Open-ended questions stimulate learners to reflect, analyze, and develop new insights by combining information they already have with new information provided by you.

Make the learner comfortable. Ask open-ended questions that put the learner in a receptive mood for learning. Be friendly and sincere. Find opportunities to compliment members and build respect within the team. Help the team members build confidence in themselves. Don't ask questions that put the participant on the defensive.

Build up the learner, not your ego.

Don't ask someone who is distracted a question. Don't throw out a question and then call an inattentive or sleepy member by name. If you want to draw one of the leaners back into the discussion, call him by name first and then restate the question.

Listen with your mouth closed. As the Manager of Learning, perhaps the most difficult technique to master is one of the most effective—having planted a seed that has gotten a response, learning to listen with your mouth firmly closed. Be patient and prepared to listen. Sometimes learners give only part of an answer. Respond patiently and encourage further thought.

Even if time is running out, avoid cutting off a person who is answering a question off unless their answer is way off target. If necessary, interrupt them politely. Say, "Arial, that's not quite what I'm looking for. Does anyone else have an idea?"

If you feel impatient, you should evaluate whether you're presenting too much information for the time available.

Wait for answers

Sometimes your open-ended question floats out over the team like a helium balloon, kept aloft by blank looks and vacant stares. Don't press the panic button. Give learners time to think! Research has shown that by pausing for only five seconds, the quality and quantity of answers actually increases.

List two ways to respond to unanswered questions.

If after five to ten seconds has gone by, here are ways to respond to unanswered questions:

Ask more specific questions. Follow up with more specific questions. Help participants to reason the problem through. The gap between the known and unknown must not be too great. You must narrow the gap so the learner's mind can bridge it. Most people think like they walk— one step at a time. Keep this in mind when using questions to tie in new information with the old. The new idea must be the next logical step. If it isn't, the learner stumbles and turns back.

Rephrase the question. Be sure that your question is clear and concise and that your manner or attitude is friendly, not unintentionally patronizing or antagonistic. Pause, look over the team slowly, and repeat, or better yet, rephrase the question. Give them time to answer. Look for someone whose body language indicates they might have an answer. Let your gaze come to rest on him. Usually he has something to say.

Give the information needed. When it becomes obvious that the learners can't answer your question, don't confuse them with more questions. Give the information needed and proceed.

Avoid negative questions. Don't ask patronizing or antagonistic questions. Don't "put someone in their place." Avoid sarcasm and forced attempts at humor. These are all inappropriate for a learning environment. They hurt people's feelings, discourage participation, and stain your relationship with them.

Don't ask someone who is distracted a question. Avoid throwing out a question and then calling on an inattentive or sleepy member by name. Avoid embarrassing someone by calling on them to expose the fact they aren't listening. If you want to draw one of the learners back into the discussion, call him by name first and *then* restate the question.

Use the Socratic Method

Asking questions is an effective—and ancient—method of managing a learning situation. The Greek philosopher Socrates proposed a dialogue between teacher and student. The teacher presents thought-provoking questions. The learners respond by asking questions of their own. The discussion goes back and forth.

The purpose is to probe learner's underlying reasoning that they rely on to make decisions and assumptions about their world. The purpose isn't to obtain a single answer, but to uncover the value system underlying their beliefs, decisions, and actions.

The Socratic Method doesn't give a learner information, knowledge, or skill except in thinking. However, the skilled Manager of Learning may use this method to encourage learners to build connections, understand responsibilities, or examine attitudes—intangible issues that are often difficult to discuss.

Five principles of presenting

These five laws of presenting are principles that help ensure that learning takes place.

List three characteristics of an effective Manager of Learning.

Characteristics of a person who is an effective Manager of Learning include:

Know the subject matter. Manage the learning process without hesitation, to improvise, and to respond to unexpected questions.

Arouse the learner to attend with interest. Design learning activities that stimulate the learner to think and ask questions.

Make the information accessible to everyone. Along with using vocabulary that everyone understands, use pictures, diagrams, charts, or even action...

Create a learning process. Help the learner move from the known to the unknown. Begin your learning process based on what the learners currently know.

Validate that learning is taking place. Participants should be actively engaged in the learning experience.

Call learners by name. Learn each participant's name and use it often. People love to hear their name and feel valued and appreciated when you remember it.

Once you gain their attention, help them form a cohesive team.

Manage the learning experience

Encourage participation. Make the learner an active partner in the learning adventure.

Involve their senses. Pour information into learners through as many inlets as possible. Create feedback loops in which the learners are participants.

Use stories. Use stories, metaphors, or analogies that the user remembers and can relate to.

Summarize. Summarize what you said so the learner can refresh what he learned.

Introduction

Get the learner's attention. Spark his interest in the subject by telling a brief story, adding background lore or history, talking about the usefulness of the information, or an exciting example of how you have put it to work. Direct questions at learners that help reveal what they already know, or that help him to think about the topic.

Explanation

Tell him about it. Include description of pertinent facts. Use charts or diagrams along with discussion if appropriate. Explain why, and perhaps emphasize details that make for success or failure.

Demonstration

Show him how it's done. Actually perform the skill; use the tool; make the widget. The explanation and demonstration often blend and overlap. The extent to which you can separate them allows you to cover the same points in two different ways, reinforcing your presentation. Concentrate on the details that make for success. Confine the demonstration and explanation to essential facts. Delay extra details or "window dressing" until the learner understands the basic skill.

Application

Have him do it. Hearing and seeing aren't enough, no matter how cleverly presented. To learn, a person must DO, preferably under their guidance and coaching of the manager of learning.

Summary

Review what he has learned. Repeat the significant details to emphasize the pertinent points, answer questions, and where feasible, have the learner turn around and help another person learn the same skill. When someone helps others learn, you know the learning cycle is successful.

Use learning time effectively

To help people remember what you want them to learn, engage them in a way that compliments their ability to remember information. Unfortunately, most instructors spend a disproportionate amount of their time talking.

Psychologists report that people remember:

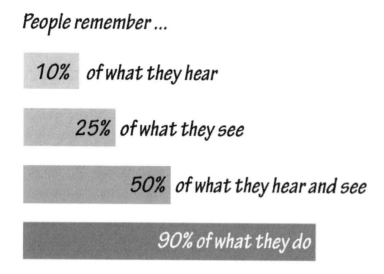

People remember ...

10% *of what they hear*

25% *of what they see*

50% *of what they hear and see*

90% of what they do

People remember more when they use their hands.

To be effective, put the majority of your time into activities that engage the learner. As a Manager of Learner, prioritize the amount of time given to participatory activities.

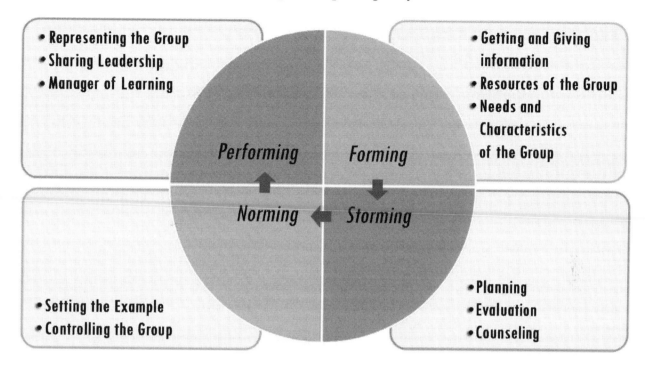

Comparing the amount of time spent communicating information using traditional instructional methods to the Manager of Learning teach / learn methodology.

More action and less talk produce greater success and longer-lasting impact for learners.

Discussion check

An effective discussion leader involves and motivates the team. To assess your success, check the following statements that are true.

☐ Team members address me as informally as they do others in the team.

☐ Members frequently show real feelings.

☐ At times members openly disagree with me and other members.

☐ Members usually address remarks to each other instead of to me as leader.

☐ The team is reluctant to quit discussing a subject when time is up.

☐ Members speak up without asking your permission.

☐ Bright ideas come from many members of the team.

☐ Members don't wait for me to cope with "problem" members.

☐ Different members lead the team's thinking and discussion.

☐ Members listen to each other without interrupting.

☐ Disagreements arise, but members deal with them objectively.

☐ Members use each other's' insights and information.

☐ Members draw reluctant or shy members into participation.

☐ Members aren't hostile or especially reserved toward me.

Application

While the concept of an application is simple, and this description is short, the application is essential to your learning activities' success.

List four principles of an effective application phase.

A few principles of an effective application phase include:

Closed the gap. At its essence, the application confirms that the learners "closed the gap" between the guided discovery and your objectives. If possible, devise challenging, hands-on situations that simulate or parallel conditions the learner may encounter in the home environment. Engage the learners in an activity that requires them to apply what they've learned. Assess how well the learner is able to apply the new principles, concepts, skills or techniques. Now compare the learners' performance during the guided discovery to the application.

Demonstrates success. The learner is able to compare what he knew before to what he knows now. He evaluates his own progress. The application is the learner's chance to put to work what you helped them learn. It's a hands-on test of your success as a Manager of Learning. The application validates that the learners gained from the learning experience.

Suitable to the learning objectives. Choose a learning activity for the application that is suitable to your learning objectives. If the learners completed terribly little of the guided discovery learning activity, consider reusing it.

Iterate and recycle. Be ready to expand any point in your presentation, based on the needs of the learners, to ensure that learning is taking place. Evaluation is continuous and so is learning. Learning takes place or is reinforced in all phases.

Evaluation

Evaluation simply means asking learners whether they have it now. Most of us are familiar with a system in which a teacher presents a subject in a lecture. They follow this with a test, which the teacher uses to evaluate your performance, often based on the dreaded "curve" that can penalize high-achievers. The evaluation for a Manager of Learning is open and doesn't penalize anyone for what they didn't learn.

Review the learning objectives. Ask the learners to evaluate their own progress. You have probably already discovered that only a few participants completed every objective. Find out if they feel the objectives were appropriate to them. Maybe you aimed too low—or high. If time permits, it may be appropriate during the evaluation to recycle and help every learner to complete the learning objectives.

Assess the learning activities and experiences. Ask the learners to give you feedback on the learning activities you chose. Find out what they think of the methods you used during the teach / learn. There is always room for correction and improvement, so be prepared to take notes.

A better alternative is to ask another staff member to watch as you conduct the Manager of Learning session. This is an effective way to help you evaluate your performance. Ask the staff member to watch for unconscious nerve janglers such as key jingling, pocket fluffing, ear pulling, marker juggling, bead flipping, knuckle popping, spectacle polishing, or gum chewing. Sometime later you will do the same for him...with pleasure.

Evaluation isn't the end of learning—it is the next step in a cyclical, ongoing learning process.

Apply it at home. The real test of the success of your leadership development program isn't what happens during the learning program itself. It's what participants' do with what they learned at home. This occurs when the trainee returns to his sponsoring home group and takes up his leadership role.

For complete information, see *Evaluation* on page 99.

Perform

Congratulations. After a number of weeks and months, you've transformed a bunch of people who didn't probably know each other well into an integrated, collaborative, high-performing team. Your biggest challenge lies ahead: take what you've learned and apply it at home, in your school, and in your community—every day.

Characteristics of high-performing teams

Over the span of several months, your group has made progress. You started out as friends and strangers with something in common. Maybe it was just membership in the same organization. You've evolved into a team that sets ambitious goals and works hard together.

List four characteristics of high-performance teams.

Characteristics of high-performing teams include:

Strong sense of belonging. Team members enjoy working together and find satisfaction in their accomplishments. They strongly identify with their team and its goals. Individuals who are happy and excited about being part of a team can achieve superior results. Team members who experience this degree of satisfaction are more likely to feel committed to the team's goals and willing to work harder and longer to help achieve those goals.

Strong leader communication. A leader who clearly communicates the team's vision, goals, and values has been shown to be highly influential in developing high-achieving teams. Leaders who continually communicate with team members about the team's vision and mission and stay in touch with team members build stronger teams.

Strong team communication. Frequent, purposeful, and short team meetings are characteristic of high-performing teams. Team communication is essential. When members are in continual contact, they're able to check on one another's progress towards goals and to recognize and applaud one another's achievements. Teams who work closely together, who stay in touch, and meet spontaneously as needed to resolve issues are more likely to succeed. Teams with clearly articulated goals and objectives are more likely to know where they stand when compared to the benchmarks and work harder to achieve those goals.

Strong team ownership. Members are proud to be part of the team. They express it in songs, yells, and cheers. Team members who contribute to defining the organization's goals and objectives feel greater commitment and ownership. They see a relationship between personal achievement and team success. They're willing to work together and are involved where ever they can contribute. Team members expect to be challenged and prefer to work hard. They expect to make sacrifices for the sake of the team.

Work in isolated locations. Teams that are isolated tend to perform at a higher level than teams whose members constantly interact with other teams. When your youth staff gets together only once or twice a month, they're focused on their goals and objectives. The time they work together in close proximity helps to remove barriers to interpersonal communication. It makes it easier for team members to collaborate and resolve challenges.

Engage in ongoing team-building activities. High-performance teams engage in formal and informal team-building activities, including formalized seminars, experiential activities, and team challenges. To help your team pull together and become more united and engaged, engage them in specific types of activities that require them to work together. Continue these activities throughout staff development.

Recognize and reward team members. High-performance teams recognize and reward team members. Individuals are usually not singled out, instead the entire team is recognized. Token rewards, including phase-specific totems, hats, and even food contribute to members' identification with the team's success.

Develop a plan to perform

When your team has achieved the performing stage of group maturity, you're ready to put your skills to work in the community.

List two ways the learner can take home what they've learned.

Learners need to apply what they've learned. Options to apply what they learn include:

At home, in real life. During each learning experience, require participants to write down ideas about how they might use what they are learning in real life, in their home, church group, leadership council, youth group or Scout troop. These are sometimes called *Leadership Growth Agreements*. Encourage participants to define how they plan to apply what they learned during your program when they return home.

Review their notes. Before your program ends, give the learners time to review their notes and develop a simple plan to apply what they've learned. Make sure they add two or three criteria that tells them when their application is a success.

The goal is to help the learner put what they've learned about leadership to work at home. As a teenager, it might be hard for them to find a leadership role. One of the most important contributions a teen can make is as a servant-leader.

Post-program projects. You want to help the learner identify a simple, post-program project they will use to apply what they learned. This helps make sure real learning takes place and continues the learning cycle.

During your program, help learners write a simple, concrete plan for applying the leadership skills. Guide them to develop a personal contract describing how they will apply the skills they learned from your group at home, in their church group, leadership council, or other organization.

The plan needs to be simple and easy to do. The goal is to give learners a taste of success that encourages them. For example, a younger participant might write:

I will talk to my parents about our vacation this year. With their input, I will use the five steps of planning to write a plan 10 days before we leave telling when we'll go and what we'll do each day.

But you ought to expect more from older and more mature participants. They might write:

I will meet with the person who planned last year's 4-H Harvest Dinner. I will ask him questions and with his input, list at least five parts of the dinner we want to keep, five ways to improve the dinner, and any parts we don't want to repeat next year. I will write a one-page report by July 15 summarizing what I learned and give it to the 4-H Foundation President.

These plans ought to use the SMART criteria. For more information, see *Write SMART objectives* on page 209. You might call this a *Personal Growth Agreement*. Make a copy of the plan before they complete camp to allow you to follow up afterward.

Serve as a leader

As teens, it may be hard to find a role where you are "in charge." One of the ways to make a big difference is to "manage from the middle." Find ways to serve your organization, even if you're not the designated leader.

The concept of servant leadership was first defined by Robert Greenleaf in 1970. Servant leadership is a practical philosophy that describes how group members—not necessarily the formal leader—devote themselves to meeting the needs of those they lead. Servant-leaders encourage the ethical use of power, shared decision making, foresight, listening, and empowerment. It's a significant departure from hierarchical, authoritarian, centralized systems of leadership. Greenleaf believed that meaningful leadership only emerges when an individual possess a deep-seated desire to first help others.

Any team member can serve the team as a servant-leader. It can be practiced at all levels in an organization. It supports people who choose to serve first and then lead. It's a way to make a significant impact on both individuals and organizations.

Servant leadership can't be readily implemented from the top down. It's not a skill that can be readily taught. It's born of a desire and an attitude within an individual who firmly desires to serve others.

It begins with the natural feeling that one wants to serve, to serve first... The leader-first and the servant-first are two extreme types. Between them there are shadings and blends that are part of the infinite variety of human nature. —Robert Greenleaf

Servant leadership isn't a specific leadership technique but a set of core personal characteristics and beliefs. A servant-leader empowers others when he helps them assume authority and responsibility to make decisions affecting their lives.

Promote community

Servant leadership promotes an experience of community where members are jointly liable for each other's well-being. It questions the organization's ability to provide appropriate and necessary human services. When team members work together they establish a community that assumes those responsibilities in a locally intensive, personalized manner unavailable to institutions.

Applying a democratic leadership principle like servant leadership to real-world organizations and situations isn't easy. Individuals often aren't open to sharing power, preferring to hold on to the authority they already possess. Adults may be unwilling to allow a teen to take on real responsibility. Adult leaders are usually trained to look for individual accountability and may not be prepared or equipped to allow teens to contribute to their organization in a meaningful way.

Community organizations and their management are often not ready to incorporate these types of processes into their effort. Some work places foster competition and not cooperation.

Ask other team members, businesses, service organizations, non-profits, and community organizations about volunteer or internship opportunities.

Put people first

Servant-leaders put the needs of team members ahead of the task. They strive to bring out the best in others and encourage self-expression. They facilitate personal growth in all around them and listen, seeking to build a sense of community and create an experience of joint ownership.

When servant-leaders are successful, they help team members to achieve their individual potential. The servant-leader helps others perform at a high level. When compared to Maslow's hierarchy of needs, servant-leaders are helping individuals achieve self-actualization. Their devotion to team members builds extraordinary team loyalty.

Servant leadership encourages everyone to work harder to value and respect others. Servant leadership is characterized by four key values.

Service to others

When an individual chooses to put others first, their primary motivation is to encourage greatness in others. The organization's success is an indirect outcome.

Greenleaf wrote that for servant-leaders, "The work exists for the person as much as the person exists for the work." The servant point of view encourages organizational leaders to treat individual success as integral to organizational success. The value put on meeting individual needs ultimately benefits the organization's long-term interests and goals.

Sharing decision making

Effective servant-leaders cultivate the same attitude and dedication in others. They nurture a collaborative, participative culture where individual contributions and success are valued. As servant-leaders encourage and help develop other team members' talents, they create a more effective, motivated team. "Leaders enable others to act not by hoarding the power they have but by giving it away."

Servant leadership turns the classic organizational pyramid on its head, putting customers, front-line staff, and others stakeholders like community members on top. Top leaders are on the bottom.

It promotes a flexible, delegated organizational structure which some behavioral scientists view as a forward-looking, post-industrial leadership model.

Characteristics of servant-leaders

R. F. Russell and A. G. Stone studied Greenleaf's work and identified ten major characteristics that characterize servant-leaders.

List two characteristics of servant-leaders.

Characteristics of servant-leaders include:

Listens. Leaders must listen with real intent to demonstrate respect for others and to sustain accurate communication. "Only a true natural servant automatically responds to any problem by listening first."

Shows empathy. Leaders who can authentically empathize with another's point of view demonstrate respect for others and build enduring and meaningful relationships. "Men grow taller when those who lead them empathize, and when they're accepted for who they are..."

Practices healing. Leaders encourage individuals to reconcile differences peaceably and with sincere forgiveness.

Demonstrates awareness. You're alert to opportunities that provide growth opportunities for individuals and the team.

Acts persuasively. The effective servant-leader uses his personal influence to build consensus. "...people are beginning to learn, however haltingly, to relate to one another in less coercive and more creatively supporting ways."

Conceptualizes information. A servant-leader is able to synthesize information and ideas and conceive of new solutions and approaches.

Exercises foresight. Effective leaders anticipate new ways to inspire team members to contribute to the entire team and organization's success. "Prescience, or foresight, is a better than average guess about what is going to happen when in the future."

A loyal steward. An effective servant-leader isn't only concerned about nurturing existing members of the organization, but looks for ways that they and the organization can impact their community in both the short- and long-term.

Committed to people's growth. You verbally shows appreciate for team member's contributions and continually encourages them. "The secret of institution building is to be able to weld a team of such people by lifting them up to grow taller than they would otherwise be."

Builds community. The servant-leader encourages team members to serve one another and their independent communities, uniting them in a common vision for the welfare and well-being of all concerned.

Of the best rulers,

The people only know that they exist;

The next best they love and praise

The next they fear;

And the next they revile.

When they do not command the people's faith,

will lose faith in them,

And then they resort to oaths!

But of the best when their task is accomplished,

their work done,

The people all remark, "We have done it ourselves."

—Lao-Tzu, Chinese philosopher, 6th century B.C.

About this Book

When I was 13, I was lost. I saw my father once a year for a day or two. My brother was in juvenile hall. My mother struggled to raise us. Eighth grade was a long, dark hallway of depression. I hated it when someone said I came from a broken family, because it was true.

But my Scout leaders saw potential in me. They invited me to the White Stag leadership camp. I wasn't sure why I was going, but I showed up. I was put into a patrol with boys I didn't know. We were all tall and lean and go-getters. At the end of the week, we were given the serious challenge to hike to the top of the Ventana Double Cone, and nothing could stop us.

We hiked up the Little Sur River, deep into the Ventana Wilderness. We repeatedly stopped and pulled out the topographic map. Laying the compass on it, we turned the map this way and that, navigating a dry, steep, chaparral-lined canyon. When the sun sunk low, we agreed–we were lost. To make matters worse, we were nearly out of water.

But our 16 year old Crew Counselor Larry Challis knew where we were, about six miles off course. What's more, he had a gallon of water in his back pack. And he didn't say a word. We threw down our sleeping bags in the middle of manzanita, beaten, and slept until dawn.

When we woke, we found a trail only a few dozen feet away. We trudged back into camp. But Larry persuaded us to learn from our mistakes. The next day our team was given a hurdle to lead the entire troop and build a 30 foot long footbridge across the river. We finished exactly on time.

That first leadership camp inspired me. I have been following the White Stag ever since. Thanks to Larry, Béla Bánáthy, Fran Peterson, Joe St.Clair, Uncle Paul Sujan, and many men like them too numerous to list, I am no longer lost. This book is my opportunity to pay it forward.